Mediterranean
Food Journey

Authentic Flavors Made Simple

SEEMA SHENOY

Copyright © 2025 Seema Shenoy. All rights reserved

No part of this book may be reproduced, or stored in a retrieval system, or transmitted in any form or by any means, electronic, mechanical, photocopying, recording, or otherwise, without express written permission of the publisher.

ISBN-13: 979-8-9924247-6-8

Cover design by: Mary de Guzman

Printed in the United States of America

To Subrao, the love of my life and my husband of 41 years—I am because you are.

TABLE OF CONTENTS

Welcome to Mediterranean Food Journey	1
The Mediterranean Mindset	2
Flavor Pairing for Mediterranean	3
The Pantry Translator	4
Meal Planning Mediterranean Style	5
Shopping Tips	6

01 MORNING & MOMENTS
Breakfast, The Sun-Soaked Way

Spanish Omelet with Potatoes	10
Avocado Toast with Fried Eggs	11
Greek Savory Pancakes with Scallions	14
Egg Whites & Feta Breakfast Wraps	15
Menemen - Turkish Scrambled Eggs	18
Green Shakshuka with Spinach	19
Greek Yogurt Parfait with Honey Granola	22
Mediterranean Omelet with Spinach & Olives	23
Artichoke Spinach Mini Frittatas	26
Egg & Cheese Breakfast Pockets	27

02 MEZZE & TAPAS
Small Plates, Big Flavors

Mini Meatballs with Herbed Yogurt Sauce	32
Crispy Chickpea Fries with Sea Salt	33
Fig & Goat Cheese Crostini with Fig Jam	36
Mushroom & Herbed Goat Cheese Tarts	37
Heirloom Tomato Caprese Bruschetta	40
Savory Chickpea Flour Pancakes	41
Pan-Fried Feta with Spiced Herb Honey	44
Roasted Red Pepper Dip	45
Spanakopita Triangles	48
Crispy Fried Olives with Garlic Aioli	49
Smoked Sardine Toasts with Orange & Mint	52
Zucchini Fritters with Herb Yogurt	53
Crispy Rice Balls with Peas & Herbs	56
Smoked Salmon Deviled Eggs	57

03 SEA & SALT
Fresh Seafood, Mediterranean Style

Rustic Seafood Stew	62
Grilled Salmon with Greek Salad	63
Cod Fritters with Red Onion & Parsley	66
Pan-Seared Halibut with Lemon & Capers	67
Shrimp in Tomato & Feta Sauce	70
Mussels in White Wine & Garlic	71
Salmon Patties with Herb Sauce	74
Sardine Pasta with Mushrooms & Peas	75
Herb & Parmesan Crusted Fish Fillets	78
Spanish Seafood Paella with Shrimp & Mussels	79
Tuna & White Bean Salad with Pepperoncini	82

04 ROOTS & LEAVES
The Heart of Mediterranean Gardens

Artichoke Soup with Lemon & Spinach	86
Caprese Panini	87
Cauliflower Shawarma Bowl	90
Light Pasta with Lemon & Garlic	91
Stuffed Peppers with Couscous & Charred Feta	94
Moroccan Carrot Lentil Soup	95
Fennel & Orange Salad with Shaved Parmesan	98
Grilled Eggplant Rolls	99
Braised Artichoke Hearts with Herbs	102
Greek Potato Gratin with Kalamata Olives	103
Stuffed Portobello Mushrooms	106
Baked Pasta with Eggplant & Tomatoes	107
Roasted Heirloom Tomato Gazpacho	110
Lebanese Green Beans in Tomato Sauce	111
Roasted Cauliflower with Chermoula	114
Arugula Salad with Pears & Blue Cheese	115
Zucchini Pasta with Basil Pesto & Burrata	118
Tuscan Ribollita Soup with Bread	119
Eggplant Parmesan on Garlic Bread	122
Pasta Salad with Roasted Vegetables	123

06 FIRE & FEAST
Hearty Mediterranean Meat Dishes

Stuffed Eggplant with Spiced Chicken	128
Grilled Lemon Pesto Chicken	129
Turkey Meatballs in Herb Cream Sauce	132
Greek Lemon Rice Soup with Chicken	133
Herb-Crusted Lamb Chops	136
Mediterranean Grain & Chicken Bowl	137
Stuffed Pork Tenderloin with Herbs & Feta	140
Turkish Pide with Spiced Chicken	141
Beef Stew with Pearl Onions	144
Ground Beef Kebabs with Vegetables	145
Moroccan Braised Chicken with Olives	148
Pesto Chicken Wrapped in Lavash	149
Sheet Pan Steak Gyros	152
Greek Chicken Souvlaki	153
Baked Cheese Tortellini with Sausage	156
Sheet Pan Garlic Butter Chicken & Potatoes	157

07 HONEY & HERITAGE
Desserts that Capture the Sunshine

Chocolate Orange Mousse	162
Honey Panna Cotta	163
Lemon Sugar Cookies with Olive Oil	166
Orange & Almond Cake	167
Honey Yogurt with Walnuts & Figs	170
Pistachio Gelato	171
Crunchy Almond Butter Stuffed Dates	174
Rice Pudding with Rose Petals	175
Baklava with Pistachios & Honey	178
Custard Pie with Figs & Honey	179

Acknowledgements	181
About the Author	182
Index	183

Welcome to Mediterranean Food Journey

Twenty years ago, I discovered something magical in my San Francisco Bay Area kitchen—the moment Mediterranean flavors met my Indian heritage, creating a culinary love story I never saw coming. I'm Seema, and what began as simple curiosity transformed into a passionate journey that has filled my home with Mediterranean sunshine for two decades.

After four decades of calling the Bay Area home with my beloved husband, I thought I knew my way around every cuisine. But Mediterranean cooking surprised me with its familiar warmth—the generous herbs, seasonal ingredients, and celebratory meals that turn every dinner into a gathering. Here was a cuisine that felt like coming home, just with new ingredients to explore.

A Love Story with Challenges

My romance with Mediterranean cooking—the way lemon brightens everything it touches, how olive oil transforms simple vegetables into something extraordinary—came with practical challenges no cookbook addressed. Living in suburban California without Mediterranean roots meant constantly asking: Where do I find sumac? Can I make tahini at home? What exactly is "good" olive oil, and how much is "a drizzle"?

These challenges led to countless kitchen experiments and a profound discovery: Mediterranean cooking isn't about having the perfect pantry or the right heritage. It's about understanding how flavors work together and embracing the joy of feeding people you love. My travels through Italy, Spain, and France confirmed this when local chefs shared their secrets—memorable meals come from love, patience, and respect for quality ingredients.

Your Journey Starts Here

If you've ever stood in a grocery store aisle, recipe in hand, wondering "How do I make this work with what's actually available to me?"—this book is your answer. It's designed for home cooks who want to embrace Mediterranean flavors without hunting down specialty ingredients or compromising on authenticity.

I've navigated every challenge you'll face and discovered practical solutions for each one. In these pages, you'll find tested substitutions, insider shortcuts, and the secrets that transformed my kitchen into a Mediterranean haven. Together, we'll make this beautiful cuisine accessible, achievable, and absolutely delicious in your own home.

Let's begin this flavorful journey together.

With love and sunshine,

Seema

The Mediterranean Mindset

Eating as Ritual, Not Routine

In our fast-paced world, meals often become fuel stops—quick, efficient, forgettable. But I found out that Mediterranean culture teaches us something profound: eating is a sacred act that deserves reverence, time, and attention.

Think about how different your relationship with food becomes when you shift from "What's for dinner?" to "How shall we celebrate this evening together?" This isn't about fancy tablecloths or perfect presentations—it's about recognizing that every meal is an opportunity to nourish not just your body, but your soul and relationships.

When I first embraced this mindset, something magical happened. My hurried weeknight dinners transformed into moments of connection. Even a simple bowl of pasta with olive oil and herbs became special when I took time to truly taste each bite, to appreciate the golden color of good olive oil, to savor the aroma of fresh basil.

SMALL SHIFTS, BIG CHANGES

- Set your phone aside during meals
- Light a candle, even for Tuesday night dinner
- Take three deep breaths before your first bite
- Ask yourself: "What am I tasting right now?"

The Art of Slow Cooking in a Fast World

Mediterranean cooking isn't about spending hours in the kitchen—it's about understanding that good things develop over time. A tomato sauce that simmers for thirty minutes tastes fundamentally different from one heated for five. Garlic that's gently warmed in olive oil creates a different flavor foundation than garlic that's quickly sautéed.

This philosophy extends beyond technique to planning. Mediterranean cooks think in rhythms: what can marinate overnight, what flavors improve with time, how yesterday's roasted vegetables become today's perfect pasta addition.

QUICK SLOW-COOKING WINS Even on busy nights, you can honor this principle. Start your garlic oil while you're putting away groceries. Let your pasta water come to a rolling boil instead of rushing it. These small acts of patience create exponentially better flavors.

Remember: you're not just cooking food—you're creating experiences, building memories, and honoring an ancient tradition of gathering around the table with gratitude and joy.

THE 15-MINUTE MEDITERRANEAN MEAL

- Keep cooked grains, canned beans, and pre-chopped vegetables ready
- Master the "bowl formula": Grain + Protein + Vegetables + Herbs + Olive Oil + Acid
- Stock quality canned fish (tuna, sardines, salmon) for instant protein
- Pre-wash and store fresh herbs in damp paper towels for week-long freshness
- Keep a jar of mixed olives and feta cubes ready for instant Mediterranean flavor

FLAVOR SHORTCUTS

- Pre-make lemon-herb oil in small jars
- Keep herb pastes frozen in ice cube trays
- Store minced garlic in olive oil (use within a week)
- Pre-mix your favorite spice blends

Flavor Pairing for Mediterranean

Mediterranean cooking isn't about complex techniques—it's about understanding which flavors sing together. Once you master these classic pairings, you'll cook with confidence and intuition, creating dishes that taste authentically Mediterranean every time.

The Magic of Mediterranean Combinations

LEMON + OLIVE OIL + HERBS
The holy trinity of Mediterranean flavor. Works on everything from grilled fish to roasted vegetables to simple salads.

TOMATO + BASIL + GARLIC
The foundation of countless dishes. Add olive oil and you have perfection.

FETA + OLIVES + OREGANO
Instant Greek salad vibes. Toss with cucumbers, peppers, or roasted vegetables.

YOGURT + CUCUMBER + MINT
Cool, refreshing, and perfect with grilled meats or as a dip.

ROSEMARY + LEMON + GARLIC
Transforms any protein. Especially magical with lamb, chicken, or potatoes.

PINE NUTS + RAISINS + HERBS
Sweet meets savory Mediterranean style. Perfect in grain salads or with roasted vegetables.

CAPERS + LEMON + PARSLEY
Bright, briny, fresh. Elevates fish, chicken, or pasta instantly.

HONEY + THYME + GOAT CHEESE
Mediterranean dessert or appetizer magic in three ingredients.

PAPRIKA + CUMIN + LEMON
Warm, earthy spices brightened with citrus. Perfect for roasted vegetables or grilled meats

OLIVES + ORANGE + FENNEL
A sophisticated combination that brings complexity to salads and grain bowls.

Quick Reference Flavor Wheel

BRIGHT & ACIDIC
Lemon, vinegar, sumac, pomegranate molasses

HERBACEOUS
Basil, oregano, thyme, rosemary, parsley, mint, dill, garlic

RICH & SMOOTH
Olive oil, tahini, yogurt, goat cheese, feta, fresh mozzarella

SALTY & BRINY
Olives, capers, anchovies, sea salt

SWEET SURPRISES
Honey, dates, figs, raisins, pine nuts, pistachios, almonds, oranges, cinnamon

WARMING SPICES
Cumin, coriander, paprika, cinnamon, allspice, za'atar

The 3-2-1 Rule To Create Any Mediterranean Dish

- Use 3 items from the same flavor family - like basil-oregano-garlic from herbaceous
- Use 2 items from a complementary family - like olive oil and feta for richness
- Use 1 surprise element - like a pinch of cinnamon or some pine nuts

The Pantry Translator

Essential Ingredients & Substitutions

THE MUST-HAVES (YOUR MEDITERRANEAN FOUNDATION)

- Extra virgin olive oil - Your most important investment
- Lemons - Fresh juice and zest are non-negotiable
- Garlic - Fresh cloves, please
- Sea salt - Coarse and fine varieties
- Dried oregano - The most versatile Mediterranean herb
- Canned tomatoes - San Marzano or high-quality whole tomatoes
- Greek yogurt - Full-fat for best results

THE NICE-TO-HAVES (LEVEL UP YOUR GAME)

- Kalamata olives, capers, tahini, sumac, za'atar, pomegranate molasses, pine nuts, feta cheese

WHEN THE RECIPE CALLS FOR → USE THIS INSTEAD

- Greek Yogurt → Regular plain yogurt strained through cheesecloth or strainer for 2 hours
- Tahini → Equal parts peanut butter + sesame oil, or make it by blending toasted sesame seeds
- Sumac → Equal parts lemon zest + paprika + pinch of salt
- Za'atar → 2 parts dried thyme + 1 part sesame seeds + 1 part sumac substitute above
- Pomegranate Molasses → Reduce 1 cup pomegranate juice with 2 tbsp sugar until syrupy
- Pine Nuts → Slivered almonds or sunflower seeds (toasted)
- Kalamata Olives → Any briny black olives (add splash of red wine vinegar)
- Feta Cheese → Goat cheese + pinch of salt, or ricotta salata (different from ricotta cheese)
- Fresh Herbs → Use 1/3 the amount of dried herbs
- Preserved Lemons → Lemon zest + coarse salt (let sit 10 minutes before using)
- Cooking Dried Beans → Canned cooked beans, rinsed with water
- Roasting Red Bell Pepper → Jarred roasted peppers
- Fresh Vegetables → Good-quality frozen vegetables

Smart Storage Tips

OLIVE OIL
Store in a dark, cool place. Buy smaller bottles.

FRESH HERBS
Trim stems, place in water, cover, refrigerate.

LEMONS
Room temperature yields more juice.

GARLIC
Store in cool, dry, ventilated areas.

NUTS & SEEDS
Freeze to extend life and prevent rancidity.

SPICES
Replace every 2-3 years. Toast whole for flavor.

Build Your Mediterranean Kit from Grocery Stores

PRODUCE SECTION
Lemons, garlic, fresh herbs (basil, parsley, mint), cucumbers, tomatoes

PANTRY AISLE
Extra virgin olive oil, canned tomatoes, dried oregano, sea salt, vinegars

DAIRY SECTION
Greek yogurt, feta, goat cheese, mozzarella

INTERNATIONAL/ETHNIC AISLE
Olives, capers, tahini, pine nuts, dried spices

Meal Planning Mediterranean Style

Weekly Sample Meal Plan: Smart Ingredient Overlap

DAY 1

- Breakfast: Greek Yogurt Parfait with Honey Granola (Page 22)
- Lunch: Arugula Salad with Pears & Blue Cheese (Page 115)
- Dinner: Grilled Lemon Pesto Chicken (Page 129)

DAY 2

- Breakfast: Avocado Toast with Fried Eggs (Page 11)
- Lunch: Fennel & Orange Salad (with yesterday's leftover chicken sliced on top) (Page 98)
- Dinner: Pan-Seared Halibut with Lemon & Capers (Page 67)

DAY 3

- Breakfast: Menemen - Turkish Scrambled Eggs (Page 18)
- Lunch: Mediterranean Grain & Chicken Bowl (using chicken from Day 1) (Page 137)
- Dinner: Herb-Crusted Lamb Chops (Page 136)

DAY 4

- Breakfast: Egg Whites & Feta Breakfast Wrap (Page 15)
- Lunch: Roasted Red Pepper Dip (using leftover herbs from Day 3) (Page 45)
- Dinner: Shrimp in Tomato & Feta Sauce (Page 70)

DAY 5

- Breakfast: Green Shakshuka with Spinach (using leftover feta and herbs from Day 4) (Page 19)
- Lunch: Greek Potato Gratin with Kalamata Olives (Page 103)
- Dinner: Grilled Salmon with Greek Salad (using remaining feta and fresh herbs) (Page 63)

DAY 6

- Brunch: Artichoke Spinach Mini Frittatas (using leftover spinach and herbs) (Page 26)
- Snack: Smoked Sardine Toasts with Orange & Mint (Page 52)
- Dinner: Turkish Pide with Spiced Chicken (Page 141)

DAY 7

- Brunch: Spanish Omelet with Potatoes (using leftover herbs from the week) (Page 10)
- Snack: Crispy Fried Olives with Garlic Aioli (Page 49)
- Dinner: Rustic Seafood Stew (using fresh herbs and lemon from the week) (Page 62)

THE MAGIC: Fresh herbs like parsley, dill, and mint flow seamlessly from Day 3's lamb through the breakfast wraps, dips, and seafood dishes. Feta cheese bridges multiple meals, while spinach appears in various forms. Lemons tie together the seafood preparations, and the herb combinations create completely different flavor profiles while using the same core ingredients efficiently.

Shopping Tips

Shop the Mediterranean Way

- Start with produce: Let seasonal vegetables guide your meal planning
- Buy multitaskers: Ingredients that work in multiple dishes (lemons, herbs, olive oil)
- Think in color groups: Red (tomatoes, peppers), Green (herbs, zucchini), White (onions, garlic)
- One protein, three ways: Buy chicken and use it grilled, in soup, and in salad throughout the week

Prep-Ahead Strategies

SUNDAY POWER PREP (30 MINUTES THAT SAVES HOURS)

- Wash and chop all herbs → Store in damp paper towels in containers, refrigerate
- Make herb oil → Blend herbs with olive oil, freeze in ice cube trays
- Cook grains in bulk → Rice, quinoa, or farro for the week
- Prep aromatics → Mince garlic, put in a sealed bag, and store in freezer

MARINADES THAT WORK OVERNIGHT

- For chicken: Lemon juice, olive oil, garlic, oregano
- For vegetables: Balsamic vinegar, olive oil, herbs
- For fish: White wine, lemon, herbs, olive oil

MAKE-AHEAD FLAVOR BASES

- Mediterranean sofrito → Sautéed onion, garlic, tomato base (freezes beautifully)
- Herb pastes → Basil-garlic-olive oil or parsley-lemon combinations
- Flavored oils → Rosemary oil, chili oil, herb-infused olive oil

Leftover Transformation Guide

YESTERDAY'S ROASTED CHICKEN BECOMES

- Chicken salad with Mediterranean herbs
- Added to pasta with olive oil and herbs
- Soup base with vegetables and grains
- Sandwich filling with roasted vegetables

SURPLUS FRESH HERBS BECOME

- Herb butter (mix with softened butter, freeze)
- Pesto variations (not just basil!)
- Herb salts (blend with coarse salt, dry)
- Ice cubes in herb oil for instant flavor boosts

EXTRA OLIVE OIL BECOMES

- Herb-infused oils for finishing dishes
- Salad dressing base with lemon and garlic
- Bread dipping oil with spices and herbs
- Marinade foundation for meats and vegetables

EXTRA COOKED GRAINS BECOME

- Tossed into pasta with olive oil and cheese
- Blended into creamy soups with broth
- Layered in frittatas or egg scrambles
- Mixed into grain bowls with fresh greens

LEFTOVER ROASTED VEGETABLES BECOME

- Breakfast bowl with yogurt and honey
- Salad base with vegetables and herbs
- Soup stretcher for heartier meals
- Stuffing for roasted stuffed vegetables

REMAINING FETA CHEESE BECOMES

- Crumbled over morning eggs and toast
- Mixed into pasta salads with vegetables
- Stuffed inside chicken breasts with herbs
- Melted into warm grain bowls

morning & moments
Breakfast, The Sun-Soaked Way

SPANISH OMELET WITH POTATOES

This vibrant Spanish omelet became my masterclass in Mediterranean patience after a memorable trip to Seville, Spain with my husband a few years back. There, I learned this technique from the chef at our hotel—Chef Enrique. When I first attempted to recreate it in my kitchen, I quickly learned what my mother always told me—that the best dishes can't be hurried. The slow cooking process that transforms simple potatoes and vegetables into this substantial, cake-like omelet mirrors the gentle approach I discovered throughout Mediterranean kitchens, where time and care create magic from humble ingredients.

Serves 4   Prep 20 mins   Cook/Bake 40 mins   Rest 5 mins

- ½ cup olive oil, divided
- 2 medium potatoes, thinly sliced
- 1 medium zucchini, sliced into rounds
- 1 red onion, thinly sliced
- 1 cup cherry tomatoes, halved
- ¼ cup Kalamata olives, pitted and halved
- 6 large eggs
- 1 teaspoon sea salt
- 1/2 teaspoon freshly ground black pepper
- ¼ teaspoon smoked paprika
- 2 tablespoons chopped fresh flat-leaf parsley
- 1 tablespoon chopped fresh oregano
- Extra herbs for garnish

COOK THE POTATOES: Heat 1/4 cup olive oil in a large oven-safe skillet over medium heat. Arrange the sliced potatoes in the skillet and cook uncovered for 10-12 minutes until tender but not browned. Remove and drain on a paper towel.

COOK THE VEGETABLES: In the same skillet, add the zucchini and red onion slices, cooking for 6-8 minutes until softened. Add the cherry tomatoes and olives, cooking for 2-3 minutes more. At this time preheat the oven to 350 °F (177 °C).

PREPARE THE EGGS: Beat the eggs in a large bowl with salt, pepper, and smoked paprika. Gently fold in the cooked potatoes, vegetables, parsley, and oregano until well combined.

START ON STOVETOP: Heat the remaining olive oil in the same oven-safe skillet over medium-low heat, pour in the egg mixture, and cook for 8-10 minutes until the edges are set.

FINISH IN THE OVEN: Transfer the skillet directly to the preheated oven and bake for 12-15 minutes until the top is golden brown and the center is completely set.

REST AND SERVE: Let it rest for 5 minutes in the skillet before cutting into wedges and serving directly from the pan.

Pair it with Tempranillo red wine, Spanish cortado coffee, or fresh-squeezed orange juice with rosemary.

Allow the cooked potatoes and vegetables to come to room temperature before adding them to the eggs. Don't rush the cooking process—slow, gentle heat on the stovetop prevents burning. Use an oven-safe skillet that goes from stovetop to oven seamlessly.

AVOCADO TOAST WITH FRIED EGGS

This dish perfectly embodies the Mediterranean philosophy I've come to love—celebrating simple, quality ingredients and transforming them into something extraordinary. The creamy avocado, golden egg, and crusty bread create the harmony that defines Mediterranean cooking: each component shines individually while contributing to something greater together. It's proof that you don't need the perfect pantry to create profound satisfaction—just quality ingredients treated with care and attention.

For the Eggs:
- 2 tablespoons butter
- 4 large fresh eggs
- ¼ teaspoon sea salt
- ¼ teaspoon pepper

For the Toast:
- 2 ripe avocado
- 2 teaspoons fresh lemon juice
- ½ teaspoon sea salt
- ¼ teaspoon black pepper
- 4 thick slices whole grain or sourdough bread
- 2 tablespoon olive oil

For Garnish:
- 4 tablespoons fresh microgreens or arugula
- ¼ teaspoon red pepper flakes (optional)
- Flaky sea salt for finishing
- Fresh herbs (your choice - chives or flat-leaf parsley)
- Extra virgin olive oil for drizzling

Serves 4   Prep 15 mins   Cook 5 mins

COOK THE EGGS: Heat the butter in a non-stick skillet over medium heat and crack the eggs into the pan. Cook for 2-3 minutes until the whites are set but the yolks remain runny. Sprinkle salt and pepper on the top.

PREP THE AVOCADO: Cut the avocado in half, remove the pit, and mash the flesh with a fork until creamy but still chunky. Season with lemon juice, salt, and pepper.

PREP THE BREAD: Toast the bread slices in a toaster or skillet until golden brown and crispy on the outside while maintaining a soft interior. Drizzle lightly with olive oil while still warm.

ASSEMBLE THE AVOCADO TOAST: Spread the mashed avocado generously over the warm toast slices, creating an even layer that covers the entire surface and extends slightly beyond the edges for an abundant appearance. (I didn't do it because it was looking messy in the picture.)

ADD THE EGGS: Carefully transfer the fried eggs on top of the avocado using a spatula, positioning so the yolk is centered and intact for a beautiful presentation when cut.

FINAL GARNISH: Garnish immediately with fresh microgreens, a sprinkle of red pepper flakes if using, flaky sea salt, fresh herbs, and a light drizzle of extra virgin olive oil before serving while the toast is still warm.

Pair it with a crisp Sauvignon Blanc, an Aperol Spritz, fresh orange juice, or Greek coffee with honey.

Choose perfectly ripe avocados that yield slightly to pressure. Toast bread just before serving for optimal texture contrast. Use medium heat for eggs to prevent rubbery whites.

GREEK SAVORY PANCAKES WITH SCALLIONS

These delightfully crispy Greek pancakes opened my eyes to the savory side of pancake-making that I never knew existed until I discovered Mediterranean cooking. Unlike sweet breakfast pancakes, these savory beauties remind me of the fritters my mother made—golden, herb-flecked, and satisfying. Fresh green onions and tangy feta create pockets of flavor that make each bite a perfect balance of crispy exterior and tender, savory interior.

Serves 4   *Prep 15 mins*   *Cook 20 mins*

- 1 ½ cups all-purpose flour
- 1 teaspoon baking powder
- 1 teaspoon sea salt
- ½ teaspoon freshly ground black pepper
- 3 large eggs
- 1 ¼ cups whole milk
- ¼ cup Greek yogurt
- 2 tablespoons olive oil, plus extra for cooking
- 1 cup finely chopped green onions (scallions)
- ½ cup crumbled feta cheese
- 2 tablespoons chopped fresh dill
- 1 tablespoon chopped fresh flat-leaf parsley
- Greek yogurt for serving
- Extra green onions for garnish

MAKE THE BATTER: Whisk together the flour, baking powder, salt, and black pepper in a large bowl. In a separate bowl combine the eggs, milk, Greek yogurt, and olive oil until smooth.

COMBINE INGREDIENTS: Pour the wet ingredients into the dry ingredients and stir until just combined. Fold in the chopped green onions, crumbled feta, dill, and parsley until evenly distributed.

COOK THE PANCAKES: Heat a non-stick skillet or griddle over medium heat and brush with olive oil. Pour ¼ cup batter per pancake and cook for 2-3 minutes until bubbles form on the surface and the edges look set.

FLIP AND FINISH: Flip the pancakes carefully and cook for another 2-3 minutes until golden brown and cooked through, adding more oil to the pan as needed between batches.

GARNISH AND SERVE: Stack the pancakes on serving plates, top with dollops of Greek yogurt and garnish with extra chopped green onions before serving warm.

Pair it with crisp Roditis white wine, Greek mountain coffee, or fresh orange juice with thyme.

Don't overmix the batter—lumps are okay and will result in more tender pancakes. Keep cooked pancakes warm in an oven at 200°F (93°C) while finishing batches. Adjust green onion amount to taste preference.

EGG WHITES & FETA BREAKFAST WRAPS

This protein-packed Mediterranean breakfast wrap transforms simple ingredients into a satisfying meal that feels both healthy and indulgent. During my years of experimenting with Mediterranean flavors, I discovered that the key is balancing textures—fluffy egg whites, wilted spinach, smooth feta, and chewy sun-dried tomatoes wrapped in soft lavash create the perfect handheld breakfast that honors both convenience and flavor.

Serves 4   Prep 10 mins   Cook 10 mins

- 2 tablespoons olive oil, divided
- 4 cups fresh baby spinach
- ½ teaspoon sea salt, divided
- ½ teaspoon freshly ground black pepper, divided
- 8 large egg whites
- ¼ teaspoon dried oregano
- 4 large lavash wraps
- ½ cup sun-dried tomatoes in oil, drained and chopped
- ½ cup feta cheese, crumbled
- 2 tablespoons chopped fresh chives (optional)

COOK THE SPINACH: Heat 1 tablespoon olive oil in a large non-stick skillet over medium heat, add the spinach and cook for 1-2 minutes until wilted. Season with 1/4 teaspoon salt and 1/4 teaspoon pepper and transfer to a plate.

SCRAMBLE THE EGG WHITES: In a large bowl lightly beat the egg whites with ¼ teaspoon salt and ¼ teaspoon pepper. In the same skillet used earlier, add 1 tablespoon of olive oil and pour in the egg whites, cooking while gently stirring for 3-4 minutes until just set but still creamy. Fold in the oregano and remove from heat.

WARM THE LAVASH: Warm the lavash in a dry skillet for 20 seconds per side until pliable, then lay flat on a work surface.

ASSEMBLE THE WRAPS: Divide the egg whites among the lavash, top with the wilted spinach, sun-dried tomatoes, and crumbled feta, then sprinkle with chives if using.

ROLL AND SERVE: Roll tightly by folding in the sides first, then rolling from bottom to top. Serve immediately or wrap in foil for a portable breakfast.

Pair it with Prosecco with fresh orange juice, cold brew coffee with cinnamon, or pomegranate juice with sparkling water.

Don't overcook egg whites—they should remain creamy for the best texture. Whole wheat tortillas are an alternative to lavash. Be sure to warm lavash/tortillas to make rolling easier.

MENEMEN - TURKISH SCRAMBLED EGGS

This beloved Turkish comfort food became one of my favorite discoveries during my Mediterranean cooking journey. The slow-cooked peppers and tomatoes create a silky base that reminds me of my mother's patient approach to building flavors—letting ingredients transform through gentle heat and time. Sweet vegetables meld into an almost sauce-like consistency while eggs are gently scrambled throughout, creating the perfect marriage of textures that defines authentic Turkish home cooking.

Serves 4   Prep 10 mins   Cook 20 mins

- 3 tablespoons olive oil
- 1 medium onion, thinly sliced
- 1 red bell pepper, deseeded and cut into strips
- 1 green bell pepper, deseeded and cut into strips
- 3 cloves garlic, minced
- 4 large ripe tomatoes, diced
- 2 teaspoons tomato paste
- ½ teaspoon sweet paprika
- ¼ teaspoon red pepper flakes (optional)
- 1 teaspoon sea salt
- ½ teaspoon freshly ground black pepper
- 6 large eggs, lightly beaten
- ¼ cup chopped fresh flat-leaf parsley
- 2 tablespoons chopped fresh dill
- Greek yogurt for serving
- Extra herbs for garnish

START THE BASE: Heat the olive oil in a large heavy-bottom pan over medium heat. Add the sliced onion and cook for 4-5 minutes until softened and translucent.

COOK THE PEPPERS: Add the bell peppers to the skillet and cook for 6-8 minutes until the peppers begin to soften. Add the garlic and cook for 1 minute until fragrant.

BUILD THE SAUCE: Stir in the diced tomatoes, tomato paste, paprika, red pepper flakes if using, salt, and black pepper. Cook for 8-10 minutes until the tomatoes break down and the mixture becomes saucy.

ADD THE EGGS: Pour the beaten eggs into the pepper mixture and gently stir with a wooden spoon. Cook over medium heat for 3-4 minutes while continuously stirring until the eggs are scrambled but still creamy.

FINISH AND SERVE: Remove from heat, stir in the fresh parsley and dill. Serve immediately from the skillet with dollops of yogurt and extra herbs for garnish.

Pair it with Turkish Riesling, Turkish tea (çay), or fresh pomegranate juice with mint.

Cook vegetables until very soft for authentic texture—they should almost melt into the eggs. Don't overcook eggs; they should remain creamy. Use the ripest tomatoes available for best flavor.

GREEN SHAKSHUKA WITH SPINACH

This vibrant green twist on beloved Middle Eastern shakshuka became my favorite after discovering how Mediterranean cooks transform seasonal ingredients into comfort food. The emerald spinach base with sweet peas creates a lighter yet equally satisfying version that celebrates spring's bounty. Building layers of flavor—from sautéed aromatics to fresh herbs and bright lemon—mirrors the patient approach I learned from Mediterranean cooks.

Serves 4   Prep 15 mins   Cook 25 mins

- 3 tablespoons olive oil
- 1 large onion, diced
- 4 cloves garlic, minced
- 1 jalapeño, deseeded and minced (optional)
- 1 cup fresh or frozen peas
- 10 cups fresh spinach - packed, roughly chopped
- ¼ cup fresh dill, chopped
- ¼ cup chopped fresh flat-leaf parsley
- 2 tablespoons chopped fresh mint
- Zest of 1 lemon
- ¾ teaspoon sea salt
- ½ teaspoon freshly ground black pepper
- 8 large eggs
- 1 tablespoon lemon juice
- ½ cup crumbled feta cheese (optional)
- Extra fresh herbs for garnish

BUILD THE BASE: Heat the olive oil in a large skillet over medium heat. Add the diced onion and cook for 5-6 minutes until softened. Add the garlic and jalapeño and cook for 1-2 minutes until fragrant.

ADD THE VEGETABLES: Add the peas and cook for 2-3 minutes until bright green. Add the spinach in batches, allowing each batch to wilt before adding more until all spinach has wilted.

SEASON THE MIXTURE: Stir in the fresh dill, parsley, mint, lemon zest, salt, and pepper, cooking for 2-3 minutes until the herbs are fragrant and well combined.

ADD THE EGGS: Create small wells in the green mixture using a spoon and crack the eggs into each well. Cover the skillet and cook for 8-10 minutes on medium-low heat until the egg whites are set but the yolks remain runny.

FINISH AND SERVE: Remove from heat, drizzle with lemon juice, sprinkle with crumbled feta if using, and garnish with fresh herbs. Serve directly from the skillet with warm pita or crusty bread.

Pair it with crisp Assyrtiko white wine, Turkish coffee, or fresh mint and cucumber agua fresca.

Use fresh spinach for the best texture as frozen releases too much water. Don't overcook the eggs—runny yolks add richness. If your skillet isn't large enough to accommodate all 8 eggs, simply divide the vegetable base between two medium skillets and crack 4 eggs into each one.

GREEK YOGURT PARFAIT WITH HONEY GRANOLA

This stunning layered parfait captures the essence of Mediterranean mornings—a philosophy I embraced after years of rushed breakfasts. The creamy Greek yogurt, golden honey, and fresh blueberries create the perfect harmony of textures and flavors that Mediterranean cooks celebrate. Each spoonful delivers contrasting elements that make simple ingredients feel luxurious, making this breakfast both nourishing and beautiful.

For the Homemade Granola:
- 2 cups old-fashioned rolled oats
- ½ cup sliced almonds
- ¼ cup chopped walnuts
- 3 tablespoons honey
- 2 tablespoons olive oil
- ½ teaspoon vanilla extract
- ¼ teaspoon cinnamon
- Pinch of sea salt

For the Parfait:
- 2 cups Greek yogurt, divided
- 1 cup fresh blueberries, divided
- 1 tablespoon lemon juice
- 4 tablespoons honey, divided

Serves 4   Prep 15 mins   Wait 30 mins   Bake 25 mins

MAKE THE GRANOLA: Preheat the oven to 325 °F (163 °C). Combine the oats, almonds, walnuts, honey, olive oil, vanilla, cinnamon, and salt in a bowl, mixing until evenly coated. Spread it on a parchment-lined sheet pan to bake for 20-25 minutes until golden brown, stirring once halfway through.

PREPARE THE GRANOLA BASE: Let the granola cool completely. Combine 1/2 cup of granola with 1/2 cup Greek yogurt in a bowl and let sit for 30 minutes until the granola softens slightly.

MAKE THE LAYERS: Mash half the blueberries with lemon juice until jammy but still chunky. Add 1/2 cup yogurt to it and mix well. Into the remaining 1 cup yogurt, add 3 tablespoons of honey and mix until smooth.

ASSEMBLE THE PARFAITS: Layer the parfaits by dividing the granola-yogurt mixture among 4 glasses, top with the honey yogurt layer, then the blueberry yogurt, and finish with the remaining granola and blueberries.

DRIZZLE AND SERVE: Drizzle the remaining honey on the top and serve immediately, or chill for up to 2 hours before serving.

Pair it with Greek mountain tea or fresh-squeezed orange juice with mint.

Make granola up to one week ahead and store in an airtight container for best crunch. Don't overmash blueberries—you want a chunky texture. Parfaits are best served within two hours to maintain granola crunch.

MEDITERRANEAN OMELET WITH SPINACH & OLIVES

This vibrant Mediterranean omelet is one of the few dishes my husband has mastered—after some trial and error, he's perfected the technique and now surprises me with it once in a while on lazy Saturday mornings. The golden eggs become a silky canvas for bold Mediterranean flavors: earthy spinach, briny olives, sweet tomatoes, and creamy feta.

Serves 4 *Prep 10 mins* *Cook 15 mins*

- 8 large eggs
- 4 tablespoons whole milk
- 1 teaspoon sea salt
- ½ teaspoon freshly ground black pepper
- 4 tablespoons butter, divided for 4 omelets
- 2 cup fresh baby spinach, chopped
- 1 cup cherry tomatoes, halved
- ½ cup Kalamata olives, pitted and halved
- ½ cup crumbled feta cheese
- 4 tablespoons chopped fresh flat-leaf parsley
- 2 tablespoons chopped fresh oregano
- Extra herbs for garnish

PREPARE THE EGGS: Whisk the eggs, milk, salt, and pepper in a bowl until well combined and frothy. Set aside while preparing the filling ingredients.

COOK THE SPINACH: Heat 2 tablespoons butter in a large non-stick skillet over medium heat, add the chopped spinach and cook for 1-2 minutes until wilted. Transfer it to a plate.

START THE OMELET: Add the 1 tablespoon butter to the same skillet. Pour in half of the beaten eggs. Cook for 2-3 minutes while gently stirring the edges to allow the uncooked egg to flow underneath.

ADD THE FILLING: When the eggs are almost set but still slightly wet on top, add half of the filling ingredients—wilted spinach, cherry tomatoes, olives, and crumbled feta—to one half of the omelet.

FOLD AND SERVE: Fold the omelet in half using a spatula, slide onto a serving plate, and garnish with fresh parsley and oregano before serving. For better presentation, I like to place the filling ingredients on top of the folded omelet—like I've done here—rather than enclosing them inside.

AND REPEAT: Repeat the process for the second omelet, or alternatively, divide the ingredients to make 4 smaller individual omelets.

Pair it with Santorini Assyrtiko white wine, Greek frappe with honey, or fresh watermelon juice with basil.

Don't overcook the eggs—they should remain creamy. Drain tomatoes and olives well to prevent watery omelet. Use room temperature eggs for best texture and easier whisking.

ARTICHOKE SPINACH MINI FRITTATAS

These elegant individual frittatas transformed my approach to breakfast entertaining after I realized that serving perfectly portioned dishes makes everyone feel special and cared for. Tender artichoke hearts and wilted spinach create the perfect harmony with creamy eggs and tangy feta, while individual portions ensure everyone gets the ideal bite. They're equally perfect for leisurely brunches or grab-and-go breakfasts.

Serves 6   Prep 15 mins   Bake 25 mins

- Olive oil cooking spray for muffin tin
- 8 large eggs
- ¼ cup whole milk
- ½ teaspoon sea salt
- ¼ teaspoon freshly ground black pepper
- 1 cup marinated artichoke hearts, drained and chopped
- 2 cups fresh baby spinach, chopped
- ½ cup crumbled feta cheese
- ¼ cup sun-dried tomatoes, chopped
- 2 tablespoons chopped fresh basil
- 1 tablespoon chopped fresh oregano
- 2 cloves garlic, minced
- ¼ cup grated Parmesan cheese
- Extra herbs for garnish

PREPARE THE OVEN AND PAN: Preheat the oven to 375 °F (191 °C). Generously grease a 12-cup muffin tin with cooking spray to prevent sticking.

MAKE THE EGG MIXTURE: Whisk the eggs, milk, salt, and pepper in a large bowl until well combined. Stir in the chopped artichoke hearts, spinach, feta, sun-dried tomatoes, basil, oregano, and garlic.

FILL AND TOP: Divide the mixture evenly among the muffin cups, filling each about ¾ full, then sprinkle the tops with grated Parmesan cheese.

BAKE THE FRITTATAS: Bake for 20-25 minutes until the centers are set and the tops are lightly golden—a toothpick inserted in the center should come out clean. Cool in the pan for 5 minutes before running a knife around the edges to loosen.

GARNISH AND SERVE: Carefully remove the frittatas from the muffin tin, garnish with fresh herbs, and serve warm or at room temperature.

Pair it with Vermentino white wine, Greek Freddo espresso, or sparkling water with lemon and fresh mint.

Can substitute olive oil for cooking spray. Drain artichokes well to prevent watery frittatas. Don't overfill muffin cups as eggs will puff during baking. Store leftovers in the refrigerator for up to 3 days.

EGG & CHEESE BREAKFAST POCKETS

These golden, flaky breakfast pockets became my solution for elegant morning meals that don't require sitting down—a perfect example of how Mediterranean practicality meets indulgence. The buttery puff pastry cradles creamy scrambled eggs and melted cheese, creating handheld treats that feel satisfying. They remind me that the best breakfasts balance convenience with the kind of care that makes ordinary mornings feel special.

Serves 4   Prep 15 mins   Cook 5 mins   Bake 20 mins

- 1 sheet frozen puff pastry, thawed
- 6 large eggs, divided
- 2 tablespoons whole milk
- ½ teaspoon sea salt
- ¼ teaspoon freshly ground black pepper
- 2 tablespoons butter
- 1 cup shredded sharp cheddar cheese
- ¼ cup cream cheese, softened
- 2 tablespoons chopped fresh chives
- 1 tablespoon chopped fresh flat-leaf parsley
- Extra chives for garnish

PREPARE THE PASTRY: Preheat the oven to 400 °F (204 °C) and line a sheet pan with parchment paper, then roll out the thawed puff pastry and cut into 8 equal rectangles.

MAKE THE FILLING: In a large bowl, whisk the eggs with milk. Set aside 1/4 cup of the egg mixture to use as an egg wash later. Add salt and pepper to the large bowl and whisk to combine. Melt the butter in a non-stick skillet over low heat and scramble the eggs gently for 3-4 minutes or until just set but still creamy. Remove from heat while slightly underdone.

COMBINE THE INGREDIENTS: Stir the shredded cheddar, cream cheese, chives, and parsley into the warm scrambled eggs until the cheese melts and the filling is creamy and well combined.

ASSEMBLE THE POCKETS: Place 2-3 tablespoons of egg filling on one half of each pastry rectangle. Fold over the pastry to create pockets and seal the edges by pressing them down with a fork. Brush the tops with the egg wash that was set aside earlier.

BAKE AND SERVE: Bake for 20 minutes until the pastry is golden brown and puffed. Cool for 5 minutes before serving garnished with fresh chives.

Pair it with Albariño white wine, Italian espresso with steamed milk, or elderflower sparkling water with lime.

Don't overcook scrambled eggs as they'll continue cooking in the oven. Seal pastry edges well to prevent filling from leaking. Serve within thirty minutes of baking for the best texture.

mezze & tapas
Small Plates, Big Flavors

MINI MEATBALLS WITH HERBED YOGURT SAUCE

These elegant mini meatballs became my signature party appetizer after finding the secret through endless trial and error—the magic isn't just in the spices, but in the gentle touch that keeps them tender. The combination of fresh herbs with warm spices like cumin and coriander creates those distinctive Mediterranean flavors that I've grown to love so much. The cooling herbed yogurt sauce reminds me of my mother's approach to balancing rich dishes with fresh, cooling elements.

For the Meatballs:

- 1 lb ground lamb or beef
- ½ cup fine breadcrumbs
- 1 large egg, beaten
- ¼ cup finely minced red onion
- 3 cloves garlic, minced
- ¼ cup chopped fresh flat-leaf parsley
- 2 tablespoons chopped fresh mint
- 1 tablespoon chopped fresh oregano
- 1 teaspoon ground cumin
- ½ teaspoon ground coriander
- 1 teaspoon sea salt
- ½ teaspoon freshly ground black pepper
- 3 tablespoons olive oil

For the Herbed Yogurt Sauce:

- 1 cup Greek yogurt
- 2 tablespoons chopped fresh flat-leaf parsley
- 1 tablespoon chopped fresh mint
- 1 tablespoon chopped fresh dill
- 1 clove garlic, minced
- 1 tablespoon lemon juice
- ½ teaspoon sea salt
- Extra herbs and red onion for garnish

Serves 6   Prep 20 mins   Wait 20 mins   Cook 20 mins

MAKE THE MEATBALL MIXTURE: Combine the ground meat, breadcrumbs, beaten egg, minced onion, garlic, parsley, mint, oregano, cumin, coriander, salt, and pepper in a large bowl. Mix gently until just combined without overworking.

SHAPE AND CHILL: Roll the mixture into walnut-sized balls (about 1 1/2-inches diameter) and place on a sheet pan. Chill in the refrigerator for 20 minutes to help them hold their shape.

COOK THE MEATBALLS: Heat the olive oil in a large skillet over medium-high heat. Add the meatballs in batches without overcrowding and cook for 8-10 minutes. Turn frequently until they are golden brown on all sides and cooked through.

MAKE THE YOGURT SAUCE: While the meatballs cook, whisk together the Greek yogurt, parsley, mint, dill, garlic, lemon juice, and salt in a bowl until smooth and well combined.

SERVE: Arrange the meatballs on a serving platter. Top each with a dollop of herbed yogurt sauce. Insert a toothpick in each meatball. Garnish with extra herbs and chopped red onion.

Pair it with Côtes du Rhône red wine, Greek retsina, or pomegranate juice with sparkling water and fresh mint.

Don't overmix the meat mixture to keep meatballs tender. Chilling helps prevent them from falling apart during cooking. Make yogurt sauce up to twenty-four hours ahead and refrigerate for best flavor development.

CRISPY CHICKPEA FRIES WITH SEA SALT

These golden chickpea fries became my answer when I crave something crispy but want to honor the Mediterranean tradition of nutritious, plant-based eating. I discovered this technique during my exploration of Italian street food in Rome, where I learned about Panelle—Sicilian fried chickpea flour fritters that inspired this recipe. The contrast between the golden, crispy exterior and creamy interior creates the perfect satisfying snack that's both indulgent and wholesome.

Serves 4   Prep 10 mins   Wait 2 hrs   Cook 20 mins

- 2 cups chickpea flour
- 3 cups water
- ¼ cup olive oil, divided
- 1 ½ teaspoon sea salt
- ½ teaspoon freshly ground black pepper
- 1 teaspoon dried oregano
- ½ teaspoon garlic powder
- ¼ teaspoon smoked paprika
- Avocado oil for frying
- 2 tablespoons fresh thyme leaves
- Flaky sea salt for finishing

MAKE THE BASE: Whisk the chickpea flour, water, 2 tablespoons olive oil, salt, pepper, oregano, garlic powder, and paprika in a saucepan until smooth. Cook over medium heat while stirring constantly for 8-10 minutes until very thick and glossy.

SET THE MIXTURE: Pour the mixture into a greased 8x8 inch pan, smooth the surface, and refrigerate for at least 2 hours or until completely set and firm enough to cut.

CUT THE FRIES: Run a knife on the 4 sides to loosen the edges. Turn out the set chickpea mixture onto a cutting board. Cut into finger-sized fries about 1/2-inch thick and 3 inches long.

FRY UNTIL GOLDEN: Heat the oil to 350 °F (177 °C) in a deep pot or fryer. Fry the chickpea sticks in batches for 3-4 minutes until golden brown and crispy on all sides. Alternatively, you could spray the fries generously with oil spray and bake them in smaller batches in the air fryer at 400 °F (204 °C) for 12 to 14 minutes.

FINISH AND SERVE: Drain on paper towels. Sprinkle it with chopped thyme leaves and flaky sea salt. Serve hot while crispy.

Pair it with Sancerre white wine, Italian chinotto soda, or sparkling water with lemon slices and fresh rosemary.

Stir the chickpea flour mixture constantly while cooking to prevent lumps. Ensure the mixture is completely cool and set before cutting. Fry in small batches to maintain oil temperature and crispiness.

FIG & GOAT CHEESE CROSTINI WITH FIG JAM

These elegant crostini became my signature appetizer after discovering how Mediterranean entertaining celebrates the marriage of sweet and savory. Living in the San Francisco Bay Area, I'm blessed with access to incredible fresh figs, and this recipe showcases how simple, quality ingredients can create something truly special. The creamy goat cheese, sweet figs, and aromatic rosemary remind me of the effortless sophistication I've always admired in Mediterranean hospitality.

For the Crostini Base:
- 1 long artisan sourdough or country baguette
- 3 tablespoons extra-virgin olive oil
- ¼ teaspoon sea salt

For the Toppings:
- 8 oz soft goat cheese, room temperature
- ½ cup store-bought fig jam
- 6-8 fresh figs
- ½ cup pomegranate seeds
- Small fresh rosemary sprigs for garnishing
- 2 tablespoons honey for drizzling
- Freshly cracked black pepper
- Flaky sea salt for finishing

Serves 8   Prep 15 mins   Bake 8 mins

PREPARE THE CROSTINI: Preheat the oven to 400 °F (204 °C). Slice the baguette diagonally into 1/2-inch thick slices. Arrange the bread slices on a large sheet pan. Brush both sides with olive oil and sprinkle with salt. Bake for 6-8 minutes until golden brown and crispy, flipping once halfway through.

PREPARE THE TOPPINGS: Bring the goat cheese to room temperature for easy spreading. Wash and slice the fresh figs into 1/4-inch rounds. Have the fig jam and pomegranate seeds ready for assembly.

ASSEMBLE THE CROSTINI: Spread a generous layer of goat cheese on each toasted bread slice. Dollop about 1 teaspoon of fig jam on top of the cheese and gently spread without mixing.

ADD THE FRESH ELEMENTS: Place 2-3 fresh fig slices on each crostini. Sprinkle with pomegranate seeds, and tuck small rosemary sprigs between the fig slices for aromatic garnish.

FINISH AND SERVE: Arrange the crostini on a serving platter or board. Drizzle lightly with honey. Sprinkle fresh black pepper and flaky sea salt.

Pair it with crisp Sauvignon Blanc or Pinot Grigio, sparkling Prosecco, or a light aperitif like Aperol with soda water.

Choose figs that are soft but not mushy, with rich color and no cracks. Crostini can be toasted up to one day ahead and stored in an airtight container. Add toasted walnuts or pistachios for extra crunch.

MEZZE & TAPAS

MUSHROOM & HERBED GOAT CHEESE TARTS

These individual mushroom tarts became my obsession after discovering them during a trip to Avignon in Provence, France—just a 3-hour train ride from Paris—with my husband. We found these magical tarts at a charming bistro near the old town, and I knew I had to learn to recreate them back home. The secret I learned from the chef is patience—letting the mushrooms release their moisture and concentrate into deep, earthy flavors. Merci beaucoup—Thank you very much, Chef Auguste.

Serves 4   Prep 20 mins   Cook 18 mins   Bake 22 mins

For the Tarts:
- 1 sheet frozen puff pastry, thawed
- 4 oz herbed goat cheese, softened
- 1 egg, beaten (for egg wash)

For the Mushroom Filling:
- 2 tablespoons olive oil
- 2 tablespoons butter
- ½ medium onion, thinly sliced
- 2 cloves garlic, minced
- 1 lb mixed mushrooms (cremini, shiitake), sliced
- ¼ cup dry white wine (optional)
- 1 teaspoon fresh thyme leaves
- ½ teaspoon sea salt
- ¼ teaspoon freshly ground black pepper

For Garnish
- Fresh thyme sprigs for garnish

PREPARE THE PASTRY: Preheat the oven to 400 °F (204 °C). Line a large sheet pan with parchment paper. Cut the thawed puff pastry into 4 equal squares. Using the tip of a small sharp knife, score a border about 1/2-inch from the edges without cutting all the way through.

START THE FILLING: Heat the olive oil and butter in a large skillet over medium-high heat. Add the sliced onions and cook for 3-4 minutes until softened. Add the garlic and cook for another minute until fragrant.

COOK THE MUSHROOMS: Add the sliced mushrooms to the skillet and cook for 8-10 minutes, stirring occasionally. Cook until the mushrooms release their moisture and become golden brown. Add the wine if using, thyme, salt, and pepper. Stir well to combine.

FINISH THE FILLING: Continue cooking for 2-3 minutes until all liquid has evaporated and the mushrooms are deeply caramelized. Remove from heat to cool slightly.

ASSEMBLE THE TARTS: Spread a thin layer of herbed goat cheese in the center of each pastry square within the scored borders. Top with the mushroom mixture. Brush the beaten egg wash over the pastry borders lightly.

BAKE AND SERVE: Bake for 18-22 minutes until the pastry is golden brown and puffed around the edges. Remove from the oven and garnish with reserved herbs before serving warm.

Pair it with Pinot Noir or light Burgundy, Champagne or Crémant de Loire, or French apple cider with fresh thyme.

Use a mix of mushroom varieties for complex flavor. Cook mushrooms until well-browned and moisture has evaporated to prevent soggy pastry bottoms. If using only one type of mushroom, use shiitake.

HEIRLOOM TOMATO CAPRESE BRUSCHETTA

This play on the classic Italian bruschetta became perfect for summer entertaining when I discovered how Mediterranean cooks let peak-season ingredients speak for themselves. In the farmer's market, I was able to get incredible heirloom tomatoes. I learned the Mediterranean philosophy of simplicity—when you have perfect tomatoes, fresh mozzarella, and fragrant basil, your job is simply to showcase their natural beauty.

For the Balsamic Glaze:
- ½ cup balsamic vinegar
- 2 tablespoons honey

For the Bruschetta Base:
- 1 large Italian bread loaf, cut into 1/2-inch thick slices
- 3 tablespoons extra-virgin olive oil
- 2 cloves garlic, halved

For the Caprese Topping:
- 2 cups diced mixed heirloom tomatoes
- 8 oz fresh mozzarella, cut into small cubes
- ¼ cup fresh basil leaves, chiffonade
- 2 tablespoons extra-virgin olive oil
- ½ teaspoon sea salt
- ¼ teaspoon freshly ground black pepper

For Garnish:
- Fresh whole basil leaves
- Flaky sea salt

Serves 6   Prep 15 mins   Cook 10 mins   Bake 7 mins

MAKE THE BALSAMIC GLAZE: Combine the balsamic vinegar and honey in a small saucepan, bring to a boil, then reduce heat and simmer for 8-10 minutes until the mixture reduces by half and coats the back of a spoon, then set aside to cool.

PREPARE THE BREAD: Preheat the oven to 400 °F (204 °C). Arrange the bread slices on a sheet pan and brush both sides with olive oil. Toast for 6-7 minutes until golden brown and crispy, flipping once halfway through.

PREPARE THE CAPRESE MIXTURE: Combine the diced heirloom tomatoes, cubed mozzarella, chiffonade basil, olive oil, salt, and pepper in a large bowl. Gently toss to combine and let sit for 10 minutes to allow the flavors to meld.

FINISH THE BREAD: As soon as the toasted bread slices are out of the oven, rub each slice with the cut side of a garlic clove half. This will infuse the bread with subtle garlic flavor without overpowering the tomatoes.

ASSEMBLE AND SERVE: Spoon the caprese mixture generously onto each garlic-rubbed toast, drizzle with balsamic glaze, garnish with fresh basil leaves, and finish with a pinch of flaky sea salt before serving immediately.

Pair it with Pinot Grigio or Vermentino, Aperol Spritz, or Italian sparkling limonata with fresh herbs.

Day-old artisan bread works best as it toasts without becoming too hard. Remove the balsamic glaze from heat before it becomes too thick—if it does thicken too much, simply whisk in a tablespoon of warm water to restore the proper consistency.

SAVORY CHICKPEA FLOUR PANCAKES

These protein-rich chickpea flour pancakes came into my life when my Lebanese coworker, Zeina, brought them to an office potluck. Since I liked them so much, she told me the technique that transforms simple chickpea flour into golden, satisfying pancakes. The nutty flour paired with fresh spinach and herbs creates a nutritious and delicious combination. They're perfect for when I have guests with dietary restrictions.

Serves 4 Prep 15 mins Wait 10 mins Cook 20 mins

- 1 ½ cups chickpea flour
- 1 ¾ cups water
- 3 tablespoons olive oil, divided
- 1 teaspoon sea salt
- ½ teaspoon ground cumin
- ¼ teaspoon turmeric (optional)
- ¼ teaspoon freshly ground black pepper
- 2 cups chopped fresh baby spinach
- 2 tablespoons chopped fresh flat-leaf parsley
- 1 tablespoon chopped fresh mint
- 2 cloves garlic, minced
- ¼ cup finely diced red onion
- Extra spinach leaves for garnish
- Lemon wedges for serving

MAKE THE BATTER: Whisk the chickpea flour, water, 1 tablespoon olive oil, salt, cumin, turmeric if using, and black pepper in a large bowl until smooth. Let the batter rest on the kitchen counter for 10 minutes to thicken.

ADD THE VEGETABLES: Stir the chopped spinach, parsley, mint, garlic, and red onion into the rested batter until evenly distributed throughout.

COOK THE PANCAKES: Heat a non-stick skillet or griddle over medium heat. Brush with the remaining olive oil. Pour 1/4 cup batter per pancake and spread slightly.

FLIP AND FINISH: Cook for 3-4 minutes until the edges are set and the bottom is golden brown. Flip carefully and cook for another 2-3 minutes until the second side is crispy and golden.

STACK AND SERVE: Stack the pancakes on serving plates, garnish with fresh spinach leaves, and serve warm with lemon wedges for squeezing over the top.

Pair it with Vermentino white wine, Lebanese arak with water and ice, or fresh mint tea with honey.

Let the batter rest to allow chickpea flour to hydrate properly. Don't flip too early—wait until edges are well set. Serve with Greek yogurt mixed with chopped mint, chopped flat-leaf parsley, minced garlic, salt, and pepper.

PAN-FRIED FETA WITH SPICED HERB HONEY

This elegant Greek appetizer became my go-to showstopper after discovering it at a tiny taverna in a San Francisco neighborhood. A friendly conversation with the owner, Dimitrios, revealed that Mediterranean cooking often finds magic in contrasts—salty meeting sweet, crispy meeting creamy. Watching thick slabs of feta develop that golden crust while staying molten inside, then getting drizzled with aromatic spiced honey, taught me that sometimes the most impressive dishes are also the simplest to execute.

Serves 4 *Prep 5 mins* *Cook 10 mins*

- 8 oz block feta cheese, cut into 4 thick slabs
- 2 tablespoons all-purpose flour
- 3 tablespoons olive oil
- ¼ cup honey
- 2 tablespoons fresh thyme leaves
- 1 tablespoon fresh oregano leaves
- 1 tablespoon finely chopped fresh rosemary
- ½ teaspoon ground cinnamon
- ¼ teaspoon red pepper flakes
- ½ cup cherry tomatoes, halved
- 2 tablespoons pine nuts, toasted (optional)
- Freshly ground black pepper
- Warm crusty bread for serving

PREPARE THE FETA: Pat the feta slabs dry with paper towels. Lightly dust both sides with flour, shaking off any excess to ensure even coating.

PAN-FRY THE FETA: Heat the olive oil in a large non-stick skillet over medium-high heat until shimmering. Carefully add the feta slabs and cook for 2-3 minutes per side until golden brown and crispy.

MAKE THE SPICED HONEY: While the feta cooks, warm the honey in a small saucepan over low heat and stir in the thyme, oregano, rosemary, cinnamon, and red pepper flakes. Simmer gently for 3-4 minutes to infuse the flavors.

ASSEMBLE THE DISH: Transfer the golden feta to serving plates, arrange the cherry tomatoes and toasted pine nuts around the cheese. Drizzle generously with the warm spiced herb honey.

GARNISH AND SERVE: Garnish with the remaining fresh herbs, add a few grinds of black pepper, and serve immediately with warm crusty bread for scooping.

Pair it with Moschofilero white wine, Greek mountain tea, or ouzo mixed with cold water and ice.

Use firm, high-quality feta for best results. Don't skip the flour coating—it helps create the golden crust. Serve immediately while cheese is warm and honey is fluid for optimal texture.

MEZZE & TAPAS

ROASTED RED PEPPER DIP

I discovered this vibrant Mediterranean dip at a small bistro in Barcelona, Spain during a trip with my husband. The gracious chef there—Chef Rolando—showed me the transformative power of fire-roasted peppers, and I was captivated by how this simple technique could create such complex flavors. The idea of charring peppers until their skins blister and their sugars caramelize creates those deep, smoky flavors is brilliant. The creamy feta adds Mediterranean saltiness that perfectly balances the peppers' natural sweetness.

Serves 6   Prep 10 mins   Roast 30 mins   Wait 15 mins

- 4 to 5 large red bell peppers
- 3 cloves garlic, roasted with peppers
- ¼ cup olive oil, divided
- ½ cup crumbled feta cheese, divided
- 2 tablespoons tahini
- 1 tablespoon lemon juice
- 1 teaspoon smoked paprika
- ½ teaspoon ground cumin
- ½ teaspoon sea salt
- ¼ teaspoon freshly ground black pepper
- 2 tablespoons chopped fresh basil leaves
- 1 tablespoon chopped fresh oregano
- Extra olive oil for drizzling
- Toasted pita pieces for serving

ROAST THE PEPPERS: Preheat the oven to 450 °F (232 °C). Place the whole red peppers and unpeeled garlic cloves on a parchment paper lined sheet pan. Drizzle with 2 tablespoons of olive oil and roast for 25-30 minutes until the pepper skins are charred and blistered.

STEAM AND PEEL: Transfer the hot peppers to a bowl. Cover tightly with plastic wrap and let them steam for 15 minutes. Peel away the charred skins and remove stems and seeds. Squeeze out the roasted garlic from the skins.

BLEND THE DIP: In a food processor, combine the roasted peppers, garlic, ¼ cup feta cheese, tahini, lemon juice, remaining olive oil, smoked paprika, cumin, salt, and pepper. Process until smooth and creamy.

DRIZZLE AND SERVE: Transfer the dip to a serving bowl. Create decorative swirls on the surface with a spoon and drizzle with extra olive oil, add a final sprinkle of black pepper, and serve with warm toasted pieces of pita for dipping. Sprinkle with the remaining feta crumbles, fresh basil, and oregano.

Pair it with rosé wine from Provence, Greek Freddo cappuccino, or sparkling water with blood orange and fresh thyme.

Steaming peppers after roasting makes skin removal easier. You can substitute store-bought roasted red bell peppers in oil to save time. Store the dip covered in the refrigerator for up to five days.

MEZZE & TAPAS

SPANAKOPITA TRIANGLES

These golden spanakopita triangles were my introduction to working with phyllo pastry—one of the most intimidating ingredients I'd ever encountered in my kitchen. The paper-thin sheets seemed impossible to handle without drying and tearing. But I was determined to master this classic Greek dish. After many failed attempts and crumpled phyllo sheets later, I finally learned the secret: patience and a damp towel are your best friends when creating these crispy parcels filled with spinach, herbs, and creamy cheese.

Serves 8 — Prep 20 mins — Cook 14 mins — Bake 25 mins

For the Filling:

- 2 lbs fresh spinach, chopped (or 20 oz frozen, thawed and drained)
- 8 oz feta cheese, crumbled
- 4 oz ricotta cheese
- 2 large eggs, beaten
- 1 large onion, finely diced
- 4 green onions, chopped
- ¼ cup chopped fresh dill
- ¼ cup chopped fresh flat-leaf parsley
- 3 cloves garlic, minced
- 3 tablespoons olive oil
- ½ teaspoon sea salt
- ¼ teaspoon black pepper
- ⅛ teaspoon nutmeg (optional)

For Assembly:

- 1 package (1 lb) phyllo pastry, thawed
- ½ cup butter, melted
- 2 tablespoons olive oil

PREPARE THE FILLING: Heat the olive oil in a large skillet over medium heat. Add the diced onion and cook it until softened, about 5 minutes. Add the garlic and cook for 1 minute until fragrant. Add fresh spinach, cooking until wilted and excess moisture evaporates, about 8 minutes.

COMBINE THE MIXTURE: Transfer the spinach filling to a large bowl and let cool completely. Stir in the crumbled feta, ricotta, beaten eggs, green onions, dill, parsley, salt, pepper, and nutmeg if using until well combined.

PREPARE FOR ASSEMBLY: Preheat the oven to 375 °F (191 °C). Mix the melted butter with olive oil. Remove the thawed phyllo sheets from the package. Keep the phyllo sheets covered with a damp towel to prevent drying. Cut the phyllo sheets lengthwise into 3-inch wide strips. Brush one layer with melted butter and lay a second layer of pastry on top of it.

FORM THE TRIANGLES: Place 1 tablespoon filling at one corner of the strip and fold it into a triangle by bringing the corner over the filling. Then continue to fold in a triangle pattern, until you have wrapped the whole strip of pastry into a triangle.

BAKE UNTIL GOLDEN: Place the triangles seam-side down on a parchment-lined sheet pan. Brush the tops with the butter mixture and bake for 20-25 minutes until golden brown and crispy.

SERVE WARM: Serve warm with dollops of Greek yogurt or tzatziki sauce, garnishing the platter with fresh dill sprigs and lemon wedges for authentic Greek presentation.

Pair it with Assyrtiko or Santorini white wine, Greek ouzo with ice and water, or sparkling water with grapefruit segments and mint.

Dry olives thoroughly to prevent coating from sliding off. Maintain oil temperature for even browning. Serve immediately for best crispiness—don't let them sit.

CRISPY FRIED OLIVES WITH GARLIC AIOLI

These irresistible crispy fried olives became my new favorite appetizer after discovering them at a Spanish tapas bar. I had never imagined that olives could be fried until I tried them there. The contrast between the hot, crunchy exterior and the warm, briny center was absolutely addictive, and I knew I had to learn how to make them at home.

For the Fried Olives:
- 2 cups large pitted green olives, drained
- ½ cup all-purpose flour
- 1 large egg, beaten
- 1 cup fine breadcrumbs
- ½ cup grated Parmesan cheese
- 1 teaspoon dried oregano
- ½ teaspoon garlic powder
- ¼ teaspoon freshly ground black pepper
- Avocado oil for frying

For the Garlic Aioli:
- ½ cup mayonnaise
- 3 cloves garlic, minced
- 1 tablespoon lemon juice
- 1 teaspoon extra virgin olive oil
- ¼ teaspoon sea salt
- 2 tablespoons chopped fresh flat-leaf parsley
- Flaky sea salt and extra parsley for garnish

Serves 4   Prep 15 mins   Cook 15 mins

PREPARE THE COATING STATIONS: Pat the olives completely dry with paper towels. Set up three stations: flour in one bowl, beaten eggs in another, and breadcrumbs mixed with Parmesan, oregano, garlic powder, and pepper in a third.

COAT THE OLIVES: Dredge each olive in flour, then dip in beaten egg, and finally roll in the seasoned breadcrumb mixture, pressing gently to ensure the coating adheres well. Use one hand for wet ingredients (egg) and the other for dry ingredients (flour and breadcrumbs) to prevent clumping on your fingers.

FRY UNTIL GOLDEN: Heat the oil to 350 °F (177 °C) in a deep pot or fryer. Fry the coated olives in small batches for 2-3 minutes until golden brown and crispy all over.

MAKE THE AIOLI: While the olives fry, whisk together the mayonnaise, minced garlic, lemon juice, olive oil, salt, and chopped parsley until smooth and well combined.

SERVE IMMEDIATELY: Drain the fried olives on paper towels. Immediately sprinkle them with sea salt and extra parsley. Serve hot with garlic aioli for dipping.

Pair it with Albariño white wine, Spanish sherry (fino or manzanilla), or sparkling water with lime slices and fresh thyme.

Dry olives thoroughly to prevent coating from sliding off. Maintain oil temperature for even browning. Serve immediately for best crispiness—don't let them sit.

SMOKED SARDINE TOASTS WITH ORANGE & MINT

These flavorful toasts completely changed my mind about sardines after years of avoiding this misunderstood fish. I finally realized the secret isn't hiding their bold flavor—it's celebrating it with bright citrus and aromatic herbs that make them shine. The creamy white bean base creates the perfect foundation, and now I actually crave these combinations that once seemed so intimidating.

For the White Bean Purée:

- 1 can (15 oz) cannellini beans, drained and rinsed
- 2 cloves garlic, minced
- 3 tablespoons extra virgin olive oil
- 1 tablespoon lemon juice
- ½ teaspoon sea salt
- ¼ teaspoon white pepper

For the Toasts:

- 4 thick slices of sourdough or Italian bread
- 2 cans (4 oz each) smoked sardines, drained
- 1 large orange, peeled and segmented
- 1 small fennel bulb, very thinly sliced
- ¼ cup fresh mint leaves
- 2 tablespoons pine nuts, toasted
- Extra virgin olive oil for drizzling
- Freshly ground black pepper
- Microgreens for garnish (optional)

Serves 4   Prep 20 mins   Cook 5 mins

MAKE THE BEAN PURÉE: Combine the cannellini beans, minced garlic, olive oil, lemon juice, salt, and white pepper in a food processor. Blend until smooth and creamy, adding water if needed for spreadable consistency.

PREPARE THE TOASTS: Toast the bread slices until golden brown and crispy. Generously spread each slice with the white bean purée while still warm.

ADD THE SARDINES AND TOPPINGS: Gently flake the smoked sardines into bite-sized pieces, removing any bones. Arrange the sardines over the bean purée along with orange segments and paper-thin fennel slices.

FINISH WITH HERBS AND NUTS: Scatter the fresh mint leaves and toasted pine nuts over each toast. Drizzle with extra virgin olive oil and add freshly ground black pepper.

GARNISH AND SERVE: Garnish with microgreens if using and serve immediately while the bread is still crispy and the toppings are fresh.

Pair it with Vermentino white wine, Italian limoncello spritz, or sparkling water with tangerine slices and fresh rosemary.

Use the best quality smoked sardines for optimal flavor. Slice fennel just before serving to prevent browning. Make bean purée up to two days ahead and store it covered in the refrigerator.

ZUCCHINI FRITTERS WITH HERB YOGURT

These crispy golden fritters became my solution for the endless summer zucchini harvest from our neighbor's prolific backyard garden—they love sharing their abundant crop with us, and I love turning them into these delicious fritters that I can share right back. During a trip to Seville with my husband, a chef there—Chef Leo—taught me the secret Mediterranean cooks know—removing every drop of moisture from the zucchini is what creates those perfect crispy edges.

For the Zucchini Fritters:
- 2 large zucchini (about 1.5 pounds), grated
- 1 teaspoon sea salt
- 2 large eggs, beaten
- ½ cup all-purpose flour
- ¼ cup chopped fresh dill
- 2 tablespoons chopped fresh flat-leaf parsley
- 2 green onions, finely sliced
- 2 cloves garlic, minced
- ½ teaspoon black pepper
- ¼ teaspoon paprika
- ⅓ cup avocado oil for frying

For the Herb Yogurt:
- 1 cup plain Greek yogurt
- 2 tablespoons chopped fresh dill
- 1 tablespoon chopped fresh flat-leaf parsley
- 1 tablespoon chopped fresh chives
- 1 clove garlic, minced
- 1 tablespoon lemon juice
- ¼ teaspoon sea salt
- ¼ teaspoon black pepper
- Extra herb sprigs for garnish

Serves 4   Prep 25 mins   Cook 15 mins

PREPARE THE ZUCCHINI: Grate the zucchini using the large holes of a box grater. Place the grated zucchini in a colander, toss with salt, and let drain for 15 minutes. Squeeze out excess moisture using clean kitchen towels or paper towels until very dry.

MAKE THE HERB YOGURT: Combine the Greek yogurt, dill, parsley, chives, minced garlic, lemon juice, salt, and pepper in a bowl, mix well and refrigerate until ready to serve.

PREPARE THE FRITTER MIXTURE: Combine the drained zucchini, beaten eggs, flour, dill, parsley, green onions, garlic, black pepper, and paprika in a large bowl, mixing until well combined and the mixture holds together.

COOK THE FRITTERS: Heat the oil in a large skillet over medium heat. Scoop 1/4 cup portions of the mixture into the pan and flatten slightly. Cook for 3-4 minutes per side until golden brown and crispy, working in batches to avoid overcrowding.

SERVE IMMEDIATELY: Stack the warm fritters on serving plates, top with a generous dollop of herb yogurt, and garnish with fresh herb sprigs before serving while hot and crispy.

Pair it with crisp Albariño or Vermentino, Greek ouzo with ice and water, or sparkling water with cucumber and fresh mint.

Removing moisture from zucchini is crucial for crispy fritters—squeeze thoroughly. Adjust flour quantity based on zucchini moisture content. Maintain consistent medium heat and don't flip too early for even cooking.

CRISPY RICE BALLS WITH PEAS & HERBS

In our first home, we had wonderful Italian-American neighbors next door—the Bernardi family—who became like extended family to us. Whenever Nonna Carmelina visited from Italy, she would bring authentic recipes and endless patience for teaching. Despite not sharing a common language, we discovered we could communicate perfectly through food. She taught me how to transform leftover risotto into these crispy golden treasures. It was my first lesson in how Mediterranean cooking never wastes anything and always makes something beautiful from what you have.

Serves 6   Prep 15 mins   Wait 30 mins   Cook 15 mins

- 3 cups cooked risotto or short-grain rice, cooled
- 1 cup fresh or frozen peas, blanched
- ½ cup grated Parmesan cheese
- 2 large eggs, beaten and divided
- 2 cloves garlic, minced
- ¼ cup chopped fresh flat-leaf parsley
- 2 tablespoons chopped fresh basil
- 1 teaspoon dried oregano
- ½ teaspoon sea salt
- ¼ teaspoon freshly ground black pepper
- ½ cup all-purpose flour
- 1 ½ cups fine breadcrumbs
- Avocado oil for deep frying
- Marinara sauce for serving
- Extra herbs for garnish

PREPARE THE MIXTURE: In a large bowl, combine the cooled rice, blanched peas, Parmesan cheese, half the beaten eggs, garlic, parsley, basil, oregano, salt, and pepper. Mix until well combined. Refrigerate for 30 minutes—don't skip this step.

SET UP COATING STATIONS: Set up three stations: flour in one bowl, remaining beaten eggs in another, and breadcrumbs in a third. Shape the chilled rice mixture into walnut-sized balls using wet hands.

COAT THE RICE BALLS: Roll each rice ball in flour, then dip in beaten egg, and finally coat thoroughly in breadcrumbs, pressing gently to ensure the coating adheres well. Use one hand for wet ingredients (egg) and the other for dry ingredients (flour and breadcrumbs) to prevent clumping on your fingers.

FRY THE RICE BALLS: Heat the oil to 350 °F (177 °C) in a deep pot or fryer. Fry the rice balls in small batches for 3-4 minutes until golden brown and crispy all over.

SERVE IMMEDIATELY: Drain on paper towels, garnish with fresh herbs, and serve immediately with warm marinara sauce for dipping.

Pair it with Pinot Grigio or Soave white wine, Italian limoncello spritz, or sparkling water with lemon and fresh rosemary.

Use day-old rice for best texture and easier shaping. Chill the mixture to prevent balls from falling apart during frying. While forming the rice balls, you could place a cube of mozzarella cheese in the center.

MEZZE & TAPAS

SMOKED SALMON DEVILED EGGS

These elegant deviled eggs became my favorite way to elevate a classic American dish using Mediterranean flavors. I love how the smoked salmon, capers, and fresh dill transform regular deviled eggs into something special that always impresses my guests. It's amazing how a few quality ingredients can make such a familiar dish feel completely new.

Serves 8 *Prep 15 mins* *Cook 12 mins*

- 6 large eggs
- 3 tablespoons mayonnaise
- 1 teaspoon Dijon mustard
- 1 tablespoon fresh lemon juice
- ¼ teaspoon sea salt
- ⅛ teaspoon white pepper
- 4 oz thinly sliced smoked salmon
- 2 tablespoons capers, drained
- 2 tablespoons chopped fresh dill
- Freshly cracked black pepper
- Extra dill sprigs for garnish

PREPARE THE HARD-BOILED EGGS: Place the eggs in a single layer in a saucepan. Cover with cold water by 1-inch and bring to a boil. Remove the pan from heat and let it stand covered for 12 minutes. Remove the eggs from the water and cool completely.

MAKE THE YOLK FILLING: Carefully peel the cooled eggs. Cut them in half lengthwise. Remove the yolks to a bowl and mash it with a fork. Add mayonnaise, Dijon mustard, lemon juice, salt, and white pepper. Mix it well until smooth and creamy.

PREPARE THE SALMON TOPPING: Cut the smoked salmon into bite-sized pieces that will fit nicely on top of each egg half, keeping pieces uniform in size for consistent presentation.

ASSEMBLE THE DEVILED EGGS: Spoon a dollop of the yolk mixture into the egg white halves, creating a smooth mound. Top each with a piece of smoked salmon and 2-3 capers.

FINISH AND SERVE: Arrange the filled eggs on a serving platter, garnish with a small sprig of fresh dill, and sprinkle with freshly cracked black pepper. Scatter extra capers and dill around the platter for decoration.

Pair it with Cava or Prosecco, crisp Vermentino, or a classic Negroni Sbagliato for aperitivo hour (Italian happy hour).

To avoid green rings around yolks, don't overcook eggs and cool immediately in an ice bath. For easy peeling, start from the larger end under running water. If the filling is too dry, add more mayonnaise.

Sea & Salt

Fresh Seafood, Mediterranean Style

RUSTIC SEAFOOD STEW

My husband and I discovered this seafood stew at a small pescheria in Sanremo, a historic fishing town in Italy, right next to the docks. This little fish market cooked the fresh seafood they caught that day for lunch, and their seafood stew was incredible. With our broken Italian and their limited English, I tried to gather what I could about the process and ingredients. When we got back home, I recreated it from memory and was amazed at how close I came to that original flavor. Since then, I've made this for special occasions when I want to bring a little of that Mediterranean seaside magic to our table.

Serves 4 Prep 20 mins Cook 40 mins

For the Base:

- 3 tablespoons olive oil
- 1 medium red onion, diced
- 3 cloves garlic, minced
- 1 red bell pepper, diced
- 2 celery stalks, diced
- 1 can (28 oz) crushed tomatoes
- 1 can (14 oz) diced tomatoes
- ¾ cup dry white wine
- 1½ cups seafood stock
- 2 bay leaves
- ½ teaspoon dried oregano
- ¼ teaspoon red pepper flakes (optional)
- ½ teaspoon sea salt
- ¼ teaspoon black pepper

For the Seafood:

- 1 pound mussels, cleaned and debearded
- 1 pound littleneck clams, scrubbed
- ½ pound large shrimp with tails, peeled and deveined
- ½ pound white fish (halibut or cod), cut into chunks

For Garnish:

- Fresh flat-leaf parsley
- Fresh rosemary
- Crusty sourdough bread

BUILD THE BASE: Heat the olive oil in a large, heavy-bottomed pot or Dutch oven over medium heat. Sauté the onion, garlic, bell pepper, and celery for 8-10 minutes until the vegetables are softened and fragrant.

CREATE THE BROTH: Add the crushed tomatoes, diced tomatoes, white wine, seafood stock, bay leaves, oregano, and red pepper flakes if using it in the pot. Bring it to a boil then reduce heat and simmer for 20 minutes to develop flavors.

PREPARE THE SHELLFISH: Add the mussels and clams to the simmering broth, cover and cook for 5-7 minutes until the shells begin to open. Discard any shells that remain closed after cooking.

ADD REMAINING SEAFOOD: Gently place the shrimp and white fish chunks into the stew. Simmer for 3-4 minutes until the shrimp are pink and the fish is opaque and cooked through.

FINISH AND SERVE: Remove the bay leaves. Season with salt and pepper to taste. Ladle into large bowls and garnish with fresh parsley and rosemary. Serve immediately with lemon wedges and crusty sourdough bread.

Pair it with crisp Sauvignon Blanc or Vermentino, Italian Prosecco with fresh herbs, or Greek ouzo with ice and a splash of water.

Use the freshest seafood available and cook the same day for best results. Add delicate fish and shrimp last to prevent overcooking. Scrub clams and mussels thoroughly and discard any with cracked shells.

GRILLED SALMON WITH GREEK SALAD

This vibrant dish came about when I realized how perfectly grilled salmon pairs with the bright, fresh flavors of a classic Greek salad. The combination of rich, flaky fish with crisp cucumbers, juicy tomatoes, and tangy feta creates this amazing contrast of warm and cool, creamy and fresh. What I love most is how the salmon soaks up the olive oil and lemon juice from the salad, while the vegetables balance out the richness of the fish. It's become my favorite way to prepare salmon because every bite feels complete and satisfying.

Serves 4   Prep 20 mins   Grill/Roast 13 mins   Rest 5 mins

For the Salmon:
- 4 salmon fillets (6 oz each), skin removed
- 3 tablespoons olive oil, divided
- 2 teaspoons dried oregano
- 1 teaspoon garlic powder
- 1 teaspoon sea salt
- ½ teaspoon black pepper
- ½ teaspoon smoked paprika

For the Greek Salad:
- 3 small Persian cucumbers, sliced into rounds
- 2 cups cherry tomatoes, halved
- ½ red onion, thinly sliced
- ½ cup Kalamata olives, pitted
- 6 oz feta cheese, cubed
- 1 tablespoon pine nuts, toasted (optional)

For the Dressing:
- ¼ cup extra virgin olive oil
- 2 tablespoons red wine vinegar
- 1 tablespoon lemon juice
- 1 teaspoon dried oregano
- ¼ cup chopped fresh flat-leaf parsley
- 2 tablespoons chopped dill
- ½ teaspoon sea salt
- ¼ teaspoon black pepper

PREPARE THE SALMON: Preheat the oven to 400 °F (204 °C) and pat the salmon fillets dry. Rub the fillets with 1 tablespoon olive oil and season both sides with oregano, garlic powder, salt, pepper, and smoked paprika.

MAKE THE GREEK SALAD: Combine the sliced cucumbers, halved cherry tomatoes, red onion, olives, cubed feta, and toasted pine nuts if using in a large bowl. Toss gently to mix the ingredients evenly.

PREPARE THE DRESSING: Whisk together the olive oil, red wine vinegar, lemon juice, oregano, parsley, dill, salt, and pepper in a small bowl until well combined.

GRILL THE SALMON: Heat the remaining 2 tablespoons of olive oil in a cast iron grill pan over medium-high heat until shimmering. Place the seasoned salmon fillets in the pan and sear for 3-4 minutes until nice grill marks form.

FINISH COOKING: Flip the salmon carefully and sear the other side for 2-3 minutes to create grill marks. Transfer the grill pan to the preheated oven and cook for 4-6 minutes until the salmon flakes easily with a fork.

REST AND SERVE: Remove the salmon from the oven and let rest for 5 minutes. Meanwhile, dress the Greek salad with the prepared vinaigrette. Serve the salmon with the salad spooned over and around it.

Pair it with Assyrtiko or Santorini whites, Greek ouzo with ice and water, or pomegranate juice with fresh mint and sparkling water.

Use a well-seasoned cast iron grill pan to prevent sticking. Don't move salmon once placed in the pan until it's time to flip for optimal grill marks. If using a thermometer, the internal temperature should reach 145 °F (63 °C) for fully cooked salmon.

COD FRITTERS WITH RED ONION & PARSLEY

These golden cod fritters took me a few tries to get right—my first batch came out dark brown on the outside and completely raw in the middle. I quickly learned that the temperature control is important here, and you can't rush the process. It's equally important to gently poach the cod first, then carefully fold it into the batter without overmixing so you keep those nice flaky pieces of fish intact. The sweet red onion and fresh parsley add great flavor, creating these crispy-outside, fluffy-inside fritters.

Serves 4 *Prep 20 mins* *Cook 20 mins*

- 1 lb fresh cod fillets, skin removed
- ½ cup all-purpose flour
- ½ cup milk
- 1 large egg, beaten
- 1 teaspoon baking powder
- 1 teaspoon sea salt
- ½ teaspoon freshly ground black pepper
- ¼ teaspoon paprika
- ⅛ teaspoon cayenne pepper (optional)
- 1 medium red onion, finely diced
- ¼ cup chopped fresh flat-leaf parsley
- 2 cloves garlic, minced
- ½ cup olive oil for frying
- Lemon or lime wedges for serving
- Extra flat-leaf parsley for garnish

PREPARE THE COD: Poach the cod fillets in simmering salted water for 8-10 minutes until just cooked through. Drain and let cool completely before flaking into bite-sized pieces, removing any bones.

MAKE THE BATTER: Whisk together the flour, milk, beaten egg, baking powder, salt, pepper, paprika, and cayenne if using in a large bowl until a smooth batter forms.

COMBINE INGREDIENTS: Gently fold the flaked cod, diced red onion, chopped parsley, and minced garlic into the batter until evenly distributed without overmixing.

FRY THE FRITTERS: Heat the olive oil in a large skillet over medium-high heat. Drop spoonfuls of the cod mixture into the hot oil, flattening slightly with the back of the spoon. After 2 minutes, reduce the temperature to medium.

FINISH AND SERVE: Fry the fritters for 3-4 minutes per side until golden brown and crispy. Drain on paper towels. Sprinkle them with extra parsley and serve hot with lime or lemon wedges.

Pair it with Vinho Verde or Albariño white wine, Portuguese galão coffee, or sparkling water with grapefruit segments.

Don't overcook cod during poaching to prevent tough texture. Drain fritters well on paper towels to remove excess oil. Serve immediately while hot and crispy for the best texture.

PAN-SEARED HALIBUT WITH LEMON & CAPERS

This elegant dish became my lesson in how to cook fish without overthinking it. The key is getting a golden crust from proper searing, then finishing with bright lemon and briny capers for that classic Mediterranean flavor combination. What I love about this recipe is how restaurant-quality it looks and tastes, but it's actually quite straightforward once you understand the technique. Good fish really doesn't need much—just a hot pan, some patience, and a few perfect accompaniments to let it shine.

For the Halibut:
- 4 halibut fillets (6 oz each), skin removed
- 1 teaspoon sea salt
- ½ teaspoon freshly ground black pepper
- 2 tablespoons olive oil
- 3 tablespoons butter, divided

For the Lemon Caper Sauce:
- 1 large lemon, sliced into rounds
- 3 tablespoons capers, drained
- 3 tablespoons fresh dill fronds
- ¼ cup dry white wine (optional)
- 2 tablespoons fresh lemon juice
- 2 tablespoons butter
- ¼ teaspoon sea salt
- ¼ teaspoon freshly ground black pepper
- Extra dill sprigs for garnish

Serves 4   Prep 10 mins   Cook 15 mins

PREPARE THE FISH: Pat the halibut fillets dry with paper towels and season both sides generously with salt and pepper. Let them come to room temperature for 10 minutes while preparing other ingredients.

START THE SEARING: Heat the olive oil and 1 tablespoon butter in a large skillet over medium-high heat until the butter begins to foam and turn light golden brown.

SEAR THE HALIBUT: Carefully place the halibut fillets in the hot skillet and sear without moving for 4-5 minutes until a golden brown crust forms. Flip the fillets and cook for another 3-4 minutes until the fish flakes easily with a fork.

ADD AROMATICS: Add the lemon slices to the pan around the fish, along with capers, and fresh dill. Cook for 2 minutes until the lemon slices begin to caramelize slightly.

MAKE THE SAUCE: Carefully remove the fish to a warm platter, leaving the other ingredients behind. Add white wine if using, remaining 2 tablespoons butter, lemon juice, salt, and pepper to the pan. Swirl for 2-3 minutes until the butter melts and creates a light sauce, scraping up any browned bits from the bottom of the pan.

SERVE IMMEDIATELY: Spoon the lemon caper sauce over the halibut fillets, garnish with fresh dill sprigs and serve immediately.

Pair it with Albariño or Vermentino, dry Greek white wine with herbs, or sparkling water with cucumber slices and fresh dill.

Use the freshest halibut possible—the fish should smell like the ocean, not fishy. Don't move the fish once placed in the pan to develop a proper golden crust. Have all ingredients ready before cooking as the dish comes together quickly.

SHRIMP IN TOMATO & FETA SAUCE

This classic Greek dish became my love affair with the magic that happens when sweet shrimp meets tangy feta in a robust tomato sauce. The secret is timing—adding the feta off the heat so it softens without completely melting, creating those perfect pockets of creamy richness that make each bite irresistible. It's one of those dishes that feels like a warm hug from the Mediterranean, with flavors that just work perfectly together.

Serves 4 Prep 15 mins Cook 20 mins

- ¼ cup olive oil
- 1 large onion, diced
- 4 cloves garlic, minced
- 1 can (28 oz) crushed tomatoes
- ¼ cup dry white wine
- 1 teaspoon dried oregano
- ½ teaspoon dried thyme
- ¼ teaspoon red pepper flakes (optional)
- 1 teaspoon sea salt
- ½ teaspoon freshly ground black pepper
- 1 cup halved yellow cherry tomatoes
- 2 lbs large shrimp, peeled with tail on and deveined
- 6 oz feta cheese, crumbled
- ¼ cup chopped fresh flat-leaf parsley
- 2 tablespoons chopped fresh dill
- 2 tablespoons lemon juice

BUILD THE BASE: Heat the olive oil in a large skillet over medium-high heat. Add the diced onion and cook for 4-5 minutes until softened and translucent.

ADD AROMATICS: Add the minced garlic and cook for 1 minute until fragrant. Stir in the crushed tomatoes, white wine, oregano, thyme, red pepper flakes if using, salt, and pepper. Bring to a simmer.

DEVELOP THE SAUCE: Reduce heat to medium and simmer the sauce for 8-10 minutes until slightly thickened. Add the halved cherry tomatoes and cook for 2-3 minutes more.

COOK THE SHRIMP: Add the shrimp to the sauce and cook for 3-4 minutes until pink and just cooked through, being careful not to overcook them.

FINISH WITH FETA: Remove from heat. Scatter the crumbled feta over the top. Sprinkle fresh parsley and dill. Drizzle the lemon juice. Let stand for 2-3 minutes to allow the feta to soften before serving hot.

Pair it with Assyrtiko or Santorini white wine, Greek ouzo with ice and water, or sparkling water with lime slices and fresh oregano.

Don't overcook shrimp as they become tough and rubbery. Add feta off the heat to prevent it from completely melting. Serve with crusty bread to soak up the delicious sauce.

MUSSELS IN WHITE WINE & GARLIC

I discovered how simple steaming shellfish can be after trying this classic bistro dish at a Mediterranean restaurant in San Francisco. I was amazed by how the steamed mussels open in aromatic white wine, releasing their briny juices to create this incredible fragrant broth that was perfect for soaking up with crusty bread. When I recreated it at home, I discovered that such basic ingredients—wine, garlic, herbs—could create something that tastes so restaurant-worthy. The key is not overcomplicating what is naturally perfect.

For the Mussels:

- 4 lbs fresh mussels, cleaned and debearded
- 2 tablespoons olive oil
- 4 tablespoons butter, divided
- 6 cloves garlic, minced
- 1 large shallot, finely chopped
- 1 cup dry white wine
- ¼ cup chopped fresh flat-leaf parsley
- 2 tablespoons fresh thyme leaves
- ½ teaspoon sea salt
- ¼ teaspoon freshly ground black pepper
- ¼ teaspoon red pepper flakes (optional)

For Serving:

- 1 large crusty baguette, sliced and toasted
- Lemon wedges

Serves 4   Prep 20 mins   Cook 15 mins

CLEAN THE MUSSELS: Clean the mussels thoroughly under cold running water, scrubbing the shells and removing any beards. Discard any mussels that are cracked or open.

START THE AROMATICS: Heat the olive oil and 2 tablespoons butter in a large, heavy-bottomed pot or Dutch oven over medium heat until the butter is melted and foaming.

BUILD THE BASE: Add the minced garlic and chopped shallot to the pot. Cook for 2-3 minutes until fragrant and softened but not browned.

ADD WINE AND MUSSELS: Pour in the white wine and bring to a simmer, letting it cook for 2 minutes to reduce slightly and cook off the alcohol.

STEAM THE MUSSELS: Add the cleaned mussels to the pot, cover immediately, and cook for 5-7 minutes. Shake the pot occasionally and cook until the mussels have opened and are cooked through.

FINISH AND SERVE: Remove from heat. Discard any mussels that haven't opened. Stir in the remaining 2 tablespoons butter, fresh parsley, thyme, salt, pepper, and red pepper flakes if using. Serve immediately with toasted slices of baguette and lemon wedges.

Pair it with Muscadet or Sancerre, French pastis with ice and water, or sparkling water with fresh thyme and lemon.

Buy mussels the day you plan to cook them and store them covered with a damp towel. Don't overcook mussels as they become tough—they're done as soon as shells open. You can substitute seafood broth for the white wine, though it will change the flavor.

SALMON PATTIES WITH HERB SAUCE

These salmon patties became my favorite way to turn fresh fish into something that feels like comfort food but tastes really special. The trick I learned is hand-chopping the salmon instead of using a food processor—it keeps the texture just right, with some chunks but still holding together perfectly. The cool, creamy dill sauce and the thin cucumber strips add the freshness. I love how versatile they are—serve them on buns for a proper sandwich or skip the bread and put them over a salad for something lighter.

For the Dill Sauce:
- ½ cup mayonnaise
- ¼ cup Greek yogurt
- 3 tablespoons finely chopped fresh dill
- 1 tablespoon lemon juice
- 1 clove garlic, minced
- ½ teaspoon sea salt
- ¼ teaspoon white pepper

For the Salmon Patties:
- 1 ½ lbs fresh salmon fillet, skin removed
- ¼ cup panko breadcrumbs
- 1 large egg, beaten
- 2 tablespoons finely chopped fresh dill
- 1 tablespoon lemon juice
- 1 teaspoon Dijon mustard
- ½ teaspoon sea salt
- ¼ teaspoon black pepper
- 2 tablespoons olive oil for cooking

For Assembly:
- 4 brioche or potato hamburger buns, toasted
- 1 large cucumber, julienned into thin strips
- 1 small red onion, sliced
- Extra fresh dill for garnish

Serves 4   Prep 25 mins   Wait 30 mins   Cook 10 mins

MAKE THE DILL SAUCE: Whisk together the mayonnaise, Greek yogurt, chopped dill, lemon juice, minced garlic, salt, and white pepper in a bowl. Refrigerate for at least 30 minutes to allow the flavors to meld.

PREPARE THE SALMON PATTIES: Finely chop the salmon fillet into small pieces. Gently combine it with panko breadcrumbs, beaten egg, fresh dill, lemon juice, Dijon mustard, salt, and pepper until just mixed.

FORM AND CHILL: Form the mixture into 4 equal patties about 3/4-inch thick, handling gently to avoid overworking the fish. Refrigerate for 30 minutes to help the patties hold together during cooking.

COOK THE PATTIES: Heat the olive oil in a large skillet over medium heat. Cook the salmon patties for 4-5 minutes per side until golden brown and cooked through, being careful when flipping as they are more delicate than beef burgers.

PREPARE FOR ASSEMBLY: Toast the burger buns lightly until golden. Julienned cucumber into thin strips. Thinly slice the red onion.

BUILD THE BURGERS: Spread dill sauce on the bottom bun half. Layer the julienned cucumber, then place the salmon patty and add more dill sauce. Arrange sliced onion on top and finish with the top bun half before serving immediately.

Pair it with Sauvignon Blanc or Albariño, sparkling water with cucumber and fresh dill, or Greek mountain tea with lemon.

Use fresh salmon and chop by hand rather than using a food processor for better texture control. Chill formed patties before cooking to help them hold together. Cook over medium heat to ensure patties cook through without burning.

SARDINE PASTA WITH MUSHROOMS & PEAS

I learned how sardines can transform pasta into something really flavorful when you don't try to hide them but let their rich, briny taste become the base of the sauce. When you toss them with hot pasta and a bit of pasta water, they break down naturally and coat everything beautifully. The earthy mushrooms and sweet peas balance out the intensity of the sardines perfectly. It's one of those rustic pantry meals that feels much more special than the effort it takes to make.

Serves 4   Prep 15 mins   Cook 20 mins

- 1 lb spaghetti
- ¼ cup olive oil
- 8 oz cremini mushrooms, sliced
- 3 cloves garlic, minced
- 1 cup fresh or frozen peas
- ¼ cup dry white wine (optional)
- 2 cans (4.2 oz each) sardines in tomato sauce
- ¼ teaspoon sea salt
- ¼ teaspoon freshly ground black pepper
- ¼ cup chopped fresh flat-leaf parsley
- 2 tablespoons chopped fresh basil
- ¼ teaspoon red pepper flakes (optional)
- 2 tablespoons lemon juice
- ½ cup grated Parmesan cheese
- Extra herbs for garnish

COOK THE PASTA: Cook the spaghetti in salted boiling water according to package directions until al dente. Reserve 1 cup pasta cooking water before draining.

COOK THE MUSHROOMS: Heat the olive oil in a large skillet over medium-high heat, add the sliced mushrooms and cook for 5-6 minutes until golden brown and tender.

ADD AROMATICS: Add the minced garlic and cook for 1 minute until fragrant. Add the peas and white wine if using, cooking for 2-3 minutes until the peas are bright green and tender.

ADD THE SARDINES: Gently add the sardines with their tomato sauce to the skillet, breaking them into bite-sized pieces with a fork. Add salt, pepper, and red pepper flakes if using, cooking for 2-3 minutes. Use less salt since canned sardines are already quite salty.

COMBINE WITH PASTA: Add the drained pasta to the skillet with the fresh herbs, lemon juice, and Parmesan cheese, tossing with pasta water as needed for silky consistency. Serve immediately with extra cheese and herbs.

Pair it with Vermentino or Greco di Tufo white wine, Italian chinotto with basil, or sparkling water with lemon and oregano.

Don't overcook sardines as they'll become mushy. Use pasta water to achieve proper sauce consistency that coats each strand. Serve immediately while hot for best texture and flavor integration. You can replace white wine with seafood stock.

HERB & PARMESAN CRUSTED FISH FILLETS

After a long day visiting museums in Florence, Italy, my family and I were exhausted and ducked into a small restaurant nearby. I ordered the fish, and it was so perfectly cooked that I had to talk to the chef. At first Chef Enzo was hesitant, thinking I might be a restaurant owner, but after I assured him I was just a curious home cook, he shared his technique. The secret is creating a golden crust that seals in the fish's natural juices while adding layers of Mediterranean flavor through fresh herbs, nutty Parmesan, and crispy breadcrumbs. It's become one of my favorite ways to make simple white fish feel special.

Serves 4　　　Prep 15 mins　　　Bake 20 mins

- 4 white fish fillets (cod, halibut, or sea bass), about 6 oz each
- 1 teaspoon sea salt, divided
- ¾ teaspoon freshly ground black pepper, divided
- 1 cup fine breadcrumbs
- ½ cup grated Parmesan cheese
- 3 tablespoons chopped fresh thyme
- 1 tablespoon chopped fresh oregano
- 2 cloves garlic, minced
- ¼ teaspoon paprika
- 3 tablespoons butter, melted
- 2 tablespoons olive oil
- 2 tablespoons lemon juice
- Lemon wedges for serving
- Extra herbs for garnish

PREPARE FOR BAKING: Preheat the oven to 400 °F (204 °C). Line a large sheet pan with parchment paper. Pat the fish fillets dry and season all sides with 3/4 teaspoon salt and 1/2 teaspoon pepper.

MAKE THE HERB CRUST: Combine the breadcrumbs, Parmesan cheese, chopped herbs, minced garlic, paprika, 1/4 teaspoon salt, and 1/4 teaspoon pepper in a bowl. Drizzle with melted butter and olive oil, mixing until evenly combined.

COAT THE FISH: Place the fish fillets on the parchment paper lined sheet pan. Brush them with lemon juice. Press the herb-breadcrumb topping firmly onto the top and sides of each fillet, creating an even coating. (Note: In the photo, I only coated the top to show the contrast between the golden crust and the white fish.)

BAKE UNTIL GOLDEN: Bake the crusted fish fillets for 15-20 minutes until the fish flakes easily with a fork and the coating is golden brown and crispy.

SERVE IMMEDIATELY: Remove from the oven, garnish with extra fresh herbs, and serve immediately with lemon wedges for squeezing over the fish.

Pair it with Sauvignon Blanc or Vermentino white wine, Greek Freddo cappuccino, or sparkling water with lime and thyme.

Don't overcook fish—it should flake easily when done. Press the coating firmly to ensure it adheres well during baking. Use fresh herbs for best flavor and visual appeal.

SPANISH SEAFOOD PAELLA WITH SHRIMP & MUSSELS

The most important rule with paella is never stir the rice once you add the stock. It took me a few tries to resist the urge, but that's how you get the coveted socarrat, that crispy caramelized bottom layer that's the hallmark of good paella. The golden saffron-scented rice creates a beautiful base for sweet shrimp and briny mussels, and the whole dish comes together in one pan. Learning to trust the process and let the rice do its thing without interference was key to getting it right.

Serves 4   Prep 20 mins   Cook 40 mins   Rest 5 mins

- 3 tablespoons olive oil
- 1 medium onion, finely chopped
- 1 small red bell pepper, chopped
- 3 cloves garlic, minced
- 1 medium tomato, grated
- 1⅓ cups bomba rice or short-grain rice
- 3 ¼ cups warm seafood stock, divided
- ½ teaspoon saffron threads
- 1½ teaspoons sweet paprika
- 1 teaspoon sea salt
- ½ teaspoon freshly ground black pepper
- 1 lb fresh mussels, cleaned and debearded
- 1 lb medium shrimp, peeled with tails on
- ½ cup green peas (fresh or frozen)
- 3 tablespoons chopped fresh flat-leaf parsley
- Lemon wedges for serving

BUILD THE SOFRITO: Heat the olive oil in a 15-17 inch paella pan (or a large skillet) over medium-high heat. Add the onion and bell pepper. Cook for 5-6 minutes until softened. Add the garlic and sauté for 1 minute until fragrant. Add grated tomato and cook until it reduces and darkens. Add the rice and sauté for 2 minutes.

PREPARE AND ADD THE STOCK: Warm 3 cups of seafood stock and stir in saffron, paprika, salt, and pepper. Carefully add the warm stock to the rice. Do not stir. Keep the remaining 1/4 cup stock in reserve.

BEGIN THE COOKING: Keep the heat at medium-high until the stock starts boiling. Reduce heat to medium-low and simmer uncovered for 15 minutes. Nestle the cleaned mussels hinge-down into the rice. Continue cooking uncovered for 5 minutes without stirring.

ADD FINAL SEAFOOD: Add the shrimp and peas to the pan, pressing them gently into the rice. Cook uncovered for 7 minutes until the shrimp are pink and the mussels have opened.

CHECK FOR DONENESS: Test a few grains of rice between your fingers to check if fully cooked. If the rice is still firm and most liquid has been absorbed, add some or all of the reserve stock. Continue cooking uncovered for 5 minutes more on medium-low heat.

CREATE THE SOCARRAT: Increase heat to high for the final 2-3 minutes to create the socarrat (crispy bottom). Remove from heat and cover with foil and a clean kitchen towel. Let rest for 5 minutes before garnishing with parsley and serving with lemon wedges.

Pair it with Albariño or Verdejo white wine, Spanish sherry with ice, or sparkling water with orange slices and fresh parsley.

Never stir paella once liquid is added—this develops proper rice texture and the crispy crust at the bottom. Discard any mussels that don't open after cooking. Let paella rest for 5 minutes before serving for best flavor integration.

TUNA & WHITE BEAN SALAD WITH PEPPERONCINI

This Mediterranean salad is all about how a few quality pantry ingredients can create something really satisfying. I found out that the secret is using the best tuna you can find—packed in olive oil, not water—and letting the pepperoncini provide that gentle heat and acidity that makes every bite sing. It's one of those dishes that requires no cooking at all, just an understanding of how flavors balance and complement each other. What started as a simple pantry meal has become one of my favorite light lunches.

Serves 4   Prep 20 mins   Cook 0 mins

- 2 cans (5 oz each) high-quality tuna in olive oil, drained
- 2 cans (15 oz each) cannellini beans, drained and rinsed
- 4 cups fresh arugula
- 1 cup cherry tomatoes, halved
- 1 small red onion, thinly sliced
- ⅓ cup sliced pepperoncini
- ½ cup mixed olives (Kalamata and green), pitted
- ¼ cup extra virgin olive oil
- 2 tablespoons red wine vinegar
- 1 tablespoon lemon juice
- 1 large clove garlic, minced
- 1 teaspoon dried oregano
- ½ teaspoon sea salt
- ¼ teaspoon freshly ground black pepper
- ½ cup crumbled feta cheese
- ¼ cup chopped fresh flat-leaf parsley

PREPARE THE TUNA: Gently flake the drained tuna into bite-sized chunks, being careful not to break it up too much. Set aside in a large serving bowl.

ADD THE VEGETABLES: Add the drained cannellini beans, fresh arugula, halved cherry tomatoes, thinly sliced red onion, sliced pepperoncini, and mixed olives to the bowl with the tuna.

MAKE THE DRESSING: Whisk together the olive oil, red wine vinegar, lemon juice, minced garlic, oregano, salt, and pepper in a small bowl until well combined.

DRESS THE SALAD: Pour the dressing over the salad ingredients and toss gently to combine, being careful not to break up the tuna too much.

FINISH AND SERVE: Top with the crumbled feta cheese and chopped fresh parsley. Serve immediately at room temperature or chill for 30 minutes to allow the flavors to meld.

Pair it with Vermentino or Greco di Tufo white wine, Italian chinotto with fresh herbs, or sparkling water with lemon slices and fresh basil.

Use high-quality tuna packed in olive oil for best flavor and texture. Don't overdress the salad—add dressing gradually to taste. Can be made ahead but add arugula just before serving to prevent wilting.

SEA & SALT

Roots & Leaves
The Heart of Mediterranean Gardens

ARTICHOKE SOUP WITH LEMON & SPINACH

On a day trip to Monterey Bay, we stopped at a roadside farmer's stand where the farmer-owner proudly told me his artichokes had been picked that morning. I bought a bag without any plan for using them, but their freshness was irresistible. Back home, I turned them into this creamy Mediterranean soup with bright lemon, wilted spinach, and tangy sun-dried tomatoes. While I've made this with those farm-fresh artichokes, I've adapted the recipe to use canned artichoke hearts so you can enjoy it anytime without the prep work.

Serves 4   Prep 15 mins   Cook 30 mins

For the Soup Base:
- 2 tablespoons olive oil
- 1 medium onion, diced
- 3 cloves garlic, minced
- 4 cups vegetable or chicken broth
- 2 cans (14 oz each) artichoke hearts, drained and chopped
- 1 tablespoon lemon zest
- ½ teaspoon sea salt
- ¼ teaspoon white pepper

For the Additions:
- ½ cup sun-dried tomatoes (oil-packed), chopped
- 3 cups fresh baby spinach
- ½ cup heavy cream
- ½ cup freshly grated Parmesan cheese, plus extra for serving
- 2 tablespoons chopped fresh basil
- 1 tablespoon chopped fresh flat-leaf parsley
- ¼ cup fresh lemon juice
- Freshly cracked black pepper
- Crusty artisan bread for serving

BUILD THE SOUP BASE: Heat the olive oil in a large pot over medium heat. Sauté the diced onion for 5-6 minutes until softened and translucent. Add the minced garlic and cook for another minute until fragrant.

CREATE THE BROTH: Add the vegetable broth and chopped artichoke hearts to the pot. Bring it to a boil then reduce heat and simmer for 15 minutes to allow the flavors to meld and the artichokes to become tender.

BLEND THE SOUP: Use an immersion blender to partially purée the soup, leaving some texture with small artichoke pieces. Or transfer 1/2 the soup to a regular blender and purée until smooth before returning to the pot.

ENRICH THE SOUP: Stir in lemon zest, salt, and white pepper. Add the chopped sun-dried tomatoes and simmer for 5 minutes to heat through and combine the flavors.

FINISH AND SERVE: Stir in the fresh spinach until slightly wilted. Take the soup off the heat. Add the heavy cream, grated Parmesan cheese, fresh herbs, and lemon juice. Ladle into bowls and garnish with Parmesan cheese and freshly cracked pepper. Serve hot with crusty bread.

Pair it with light Chardonnay or Vermentino, Aperol Spritz with fresh herbs, or sparkling water with lemon and fresh basil.

Add spinach at the end to maintain a vibrant color. Soup base can be made up to 2 days ahead before adding cream and final ingredients. To prevent the soup from curdling, add lemon juice last, just before serving.

ROOTS & LEAVES

CAPRESE PANINI

This pressed sandwich happened almost by accident when I had leftover caprese salad ingredients and some bread on hand. The heat changes everything—the mozzarella melts perfectly, the tomatoes get jammy and sweet, and the basil releases its fragrance in a way that cold salads just can't match. The avocado addition came from having half of one sitting on my counter, and now I can't make this sandwich without it. That creamy texture balances the bright tomato and herbs beautifully, turning a simple combination into something more substantial and satisfying.

For the Avocado Spread:
- 1 large ripe avocado
- 1 tablespoon fresh lemon juice
- ⅛ teaspoon sea salt
- ⅛ teaspoon freshly ground black pepper

For the Sandwiches:
- 4 medium tomatoes, sliced into 1/4-inch rounds
- ⅛ teaspoon sea salt
- ¼ teaspoon freshly ground black pepper
- 8 slices of thick sourdough bread
- 4 tablespoons unsalted butter, softened
- 8 oz fresh mozzarella cheese, sliced
- ¼ cup fresh basil leaves

Serves 4   Prep 10 mins   Wait 10 mins   Grill 12 mins

MAKE THE AVOCADO SPREAD: Remove the flesh of the avocado and mash it in a bowl with lemon juice, salt, and pepper until smooth and creamy. Set aside while preparing other ingredients.

PREPARE THE TOMATOES: Slice the tomatoes and lay on paper towels. Season them on both sides with salt and let them sit for 10 minutes to draw out excess moisture. Sprinkle pepper over the tomato slices.

PREPARE THE BREAD: Spread the softened butter on one side of all 8 bread slices. Flip 4 slices and spread the mashed avocado on the unbuttered sides.

ASSEMBLE THE SANDWICHES: Layer the fresh mozzarella slices, seasoned tomato slices, and fresh basil leaves over the avocado spread. Top with the remaining bread slices, buttered side facing out.

GRILL THE PANINI: Heat a large skillet or griddle over medium-low heat. Grill the sandwiches for 3-4 minutes per side, pressing gently with a spatula, until golden brown and the cheese has melted.

REST AND SERVE: Remove from heat and let rest for 1 minute before cutting in half. Serve immediately while the cheese is still melty and the bread is crispy.

Pair it with Sauvignon Blanc or Vermentino, Italian limonata with fresh basil, or sparkling water with cucumber and fresh mint.

Choose avocados that yield slightly to pressure but aren't overly soft to prevent the spread from becoming watery. Pat tomatoes dry after salting to prevent soggy bread. Cook on medium-low heat to allow cheese to melt completely.

CAULIFLOWER SHAWARMA BOWL

I developed this recipe by taking inspiration from traditional meat shawarma and discovering how those warm Middle Eastern spices transform roasted cauliflower into something deeply caramelized and substantial. The real magic happens when the spice blend hits the heat—the cauliflower becomes incredibly flavorful and satisfying. Adding crispy chickpeas gives the bowl protein and crunch, while fresh vegetables and creamy tahini sauce round everything out. It's become one of those meals I crave regularly, not because it's healthy, but because it genuinely tastes amazing.

For the Shawarma Cauliflower:

- 1 large head cauliflower, cut into medium size florets
- 3 tablespoons olive oil
- 2 teaspoons ground cumin
- 2 teaspoons smoked paprika
- 1 teaspoon ground coriander
- ½ teaspoon turmeric
- ½ teaspoon cinnamon
- 1 teaspoon sea salt
- ½ teaspoon black pepper

For the Crispy Chickpeas:

- 1 can (15 oz) chickpeas, drained and patted dry
- 2 tablespoons olive oil
- 1 teaspoon ground cumin
- ½ teaspoon smoked paprika
- ½ teaspoon sea salt

For the Cherry Tomatoes:

- 2 cups cherry tomatoes
- 1 tablespoon olive oil

For the Green Tahini Sauce:

- ¼ cup tahini
- ¼ cup fresh flat-leaf parsley
- ¼ cup fresh cilantro leaves
- 2 tablespoons lemon juice
- 1 clove garlic
- ½ teaspoon sea salt
- 3-4 tablespoons warm water

For Assembly:

- 2 cups cooked basmati rice
- 1 Persian cucumber, sliced

Serves 4   Prep 25 mins   Roast 20 mins

PREPARE FOR ROASTING: Preheat the oven to 425 °F (218 °C). Line one large sheet pan with parchment paper for the cauliflower. On a second sheet pan, line half with crumpled parchment paper and half with flat parchment paper. The crumpled side will catch tomato juices while the flat side will keep the chickpeas dry and crispy.

SEASON THE CAULIFLOWER: Toss the florets with olive oil, cumin, paprika, coriander, turmeric, cinnamon, salt, and pepper in a large bowl until well coated. Spread the florets on the sheet pan with a single parchment.

PREPARE CHICKPEAS AND TOMATOES: In a medium bowl, toss the chickpeas with olive oil, cumin, paprika, and salt. Spread them on the flat parchment side of the second sheet pan. Halve the tomatoes. Using the same bowl, toss the halved cherry tomatoes with olive oil. Spread them on the crumpled parchment side.

ROAST EVERYTHING: Place both sheet pans in the oven. Roast the cauliflower on the upper rack for 20 minutes until golden and tender. Roast the chickpeas and tomatoes on the lower rack for 20 minutes until the chickpeas are crispy and the tomatoes are slightly caramelized.

MAKE THE GREEN TAHINI SAUCE: Process the tahini, parsley, cilantro, lemon juice, garlic, and salt in a food processor until smooth. Add warm water, as needed, until you reach a pourable consistency.

ASSEMBLE THE BOWLS: Divide the rice among 4 bowls, top with roasted cauliflower, chickpeas, tomatoes, cucumber and drizzle with tahini sauce.

Pair it with Lebanese Arak with water and ice, pomegranate juice with sparkling water, or herbal tea with rose petals.

Pat the chickpeas dry completely before roasting. Tahini sauce can be made up to 3 days ahead. Substitute rice with quinoa for more protein.

LIGHT PASTA WITH LEMON & GARLIC

This has become my weeknight lifesaver when I need dinner on the table fast but still want something that feels special. The trick is using starchy pasta water to create a silky sauce with just olive oil and garlic—no cream needed. The bright lemon and crunchy toasted walnuts add the perfect finishing touches. It's Mediterranean cooking at its simplest: good ingredients doing what they do best, and it's ready in the time it takes to boil pasta.

Serves 4   Prep 10 mins   Cook 15 mins

- 1 lb spaghetti
- ½ cup extra virgin olive oil
- 6 cloves garlic, thinly sliced
- 3/4 cup walnuts, roughly chopped and toasted
- Zest of 2 large lemons
- ¼ cup fresh lemon juice
- ½ cup fresh chopped flat-leaf parsley
- ½ cup grated Parmesan cheese, plus extra for serving
- 1 teaspoon sea salt
- ½ teaspoon freshly ground black pepper
- ¼ teaspoon red pepper flakes (optional)

COOK THE PASTA: Cook the spaghetti in salted boiling water according to package directions until al dente or well cooked, based on your own preference. Reserve 1 cup pasta cooking water before draining.

BUILD THE SAUCE: While the pasta cooks, heat the olive oil in a large skillet over medium-low heat. Add the sliced garlic and cook for 2-3 minutes until fragrant and lightly golden, being careful not to burn.

ADD THE WALNUTS: Add the toasted walnuts to the garlic oil and cook for 1 minute, then add the lemon zest and cook for another 30 seconds until aromatic. Turn off the heat.

COMBINE AND TOSS: Add the drained hot pasta to the skillet along with the lemon juice, chopped parsley, Parmesan cheese, salt, pepper, and red pepper flakes if using. Toss vigorously and add pasta water as needed for silky consistency.

SERVE IMMEDIATELY: Divide among serving bowls and serve immediately with additional Parmesan cheese and freshly ground black pepper.

Pair it with Vermentino or Greco di Tufo white wine, Italian chinotto with fresh lemon, or sparkling water with cucumber and fresh parsley.

Don't let the garlic brown or it will turn bitter. Reserve some pasta water to help create the proper sauce consistency. For variation, try adding baby spinach leaves and/or chopped sun-dried tomatoes just before adding pasta.

STUFFED PEPPERS WITH COUSCOUS & CHARRED FETA

These colorful stuffed peppers became my favorite choice when I want something that looks impressive but doesn't require complicated techniques. The key is treating the peppers like edible bowls, filling them with fluffy, herb-scented couscous that soaks up all the sweet pepper juices as everything bakes together. What I love most is how the pepper walls get tender and slightly caramelized while the feta gets charred. A simple side salad tossed with vinaigrette adds extra color and freshness to the plate.

Serves 4   Prep 15 mins   Cook 21 mins   Bake 30 mins

- 4 large red bell peppers
- 3 tablespoons olive oil, divided
- 1 medium onion, finely diced
- 2 cloves garlic, minced
- 1 cup uncooked pearl couscous
- 1 ½ cups vegetable broth, hot
- 1 teaspoon dried oregano
- ½ teaspoon sea salt
- ¼ teaspoon black pepper
- ¼ cup pine nuts, toasted
- ¼ cup chopped fresh flat-leaf parsley
- 2 tablespoons chopped mint
- 1 tablespoon chopped dill
- 4 oz feta cheese, divided
- 2 tablespoons lemon juice
- Fresh herbs for garnish

PREPARE THE PEPPERS: Preheat the oven to 400 °F (204 °C). With a small paring knife, cut off the tops and remove the seeds from the bell peppers. Brush the outside of the peppers with 1 tablespoon olive oil and place in a baking dish.

BUILD THE AROMATIC BASE: Heat remaining 2 tablespoons olive oil in a large skillet over medium-high heat. Add diced onion and sauté for 4 minutes until softened. Add garlic and cook for 1 minute until fragrant.

MAKE THE FILLING: Add the uncooked couscous to the skillet and sauté for 3 minutes on medium-high heat or until the couscous is slightly golden brown. Add the hot broth, dried oregano, salt, and pepper. Stir to combine. Reduce the heat to low, cover, and simmer for 10-13 minutes, or until the couscous is tender and all the liquid has been absorbed. Be sure to stir a couple of times in between. Fluff the couscous with a fork and mix in the pine nuts, parsley, mint, dill, and lemon juice.

PREPARE THE FETA: Crumble half of the feta and set aside for garnish. Cut the remaining half into small thin slices.

STUFF, TOP, AND BAKE: Divide the stuffing evenly among the 4 peppers, packing gently. Top each pepper with thin slices of feta cheese. Cover the baking dish with foil and bake for 15 minutes. Remove foil and bake for an additional 15 minutes until peppers are tender and feta is charred.

FINISH AND SERVE: Remove from the oven and let cool for 5 minutes. Top each pepper with crumbled fresh feta and garnish with additional fresh herbs before serving.

Pair with a crisp Sauvignon Blanc, Greek white wine, or sparkling water with orange slices and fresh mint.

Choose peppers that can stand upright. Trim the bottom of peppers slightly if needed to help them stand upright. Can be assembled ahead and refrigerated before baking.

MOROCCAN CARROT LENTIL SOUP

This soul-warming soup became my introduction to the magic of Moroccan spice blending after visiting an international spice market in the Bay Area. The owner gave me a complimentary sample of her Moroccan spice blend, confident that I was going to love it—and she was absolutely right. The way these warming spices transform carrots and red lentils into something deeply satisfying amazed me. The secret is toasting the spices until they release their essential oils, creating a fragrant foundation for the soup. If you can find a ready-made Moroccan spice blend, feel free to use it instead of the individual dry spices I've listed in the recipe.

Serves 4   Prep 15 mins   Cook 35 mins

- 1½ tablespoons olive oil
- 1 medium onion, diced
- 2 cloves garlic, minced
- 2 teaspoons minced fresh ginger
- 1½ teaspoons ground cumin
- ¾ teaspoon ground coriander
- ½ teaspoon ground cinnamon
- ¼ teaspoon cayenne pepper
- 1½ lbs carrots, peeled and chopped
- 1 cup uncooked red lentils, rinsed
- 4 cups vegetable broth
- 1 can (about 14.5 oz) diced tomatoes
- 1½ teaspoons sea salt
- ½ teaspoon black pepper
- 3 tablespoons chopped fresh cilantro
- 3 tablespoons chopped fresh flat-leaf parsley
- Greek yogurt for serving (optional)
- Lemon wedges for serving (optional)
- Extra herbs for garnish

BUILD THE AROMATIC BASE: Heat the olive oil in a large heavy-bottomed pot over medium heat. Add the onion and cook for 5-6 minutes until softened. Add the garlic and ginger, cooking for 2 minutes until fragrant.

TOAST THE SPICES: Add the cumin, coriander, cinnamon, and cayenne to the pot, stirring for 30 seconds until the spices are aromatic and toasted.

ADD THE MAIN INGREDIENTS: Add the chopped carrots, red lentils, vegetable broth, and diced tomatoes to the pot. Increase the heat to high. Bring to a boil. Reduce heat to medium-low and simmer for 25-30 minutes until the carrots are very tender and the lentils have broken down.

BLEND FOR TEXTURE: Using an immersion blender, partially blend the soup to your desired consistency, leaving some texture while creating a creamy base. Season with salt and pepper.

FINISH AND SERVE: Stir in the fresh cilantro and parsley. Ladle the soup into bowls and serve hot with dollops of Greek yogurt if using, extra herbs, and lemon wedges on the side.

Pair it with Côtes du Rhône red wine, Moroccan mint tea with honey, or fresh orange juice with cinnamon and sparkling water.

Red lentils cook quickly and break down naturally for creaminess. Reduce the heat when adding the dry spices to prevent them from burning. Can be made ahead and refrigerated for up to four days.

FENNEL & ORANGE SALAD WITH SHAVED PARMESAN

This refreshing salad came about when my favorite vendor at our weekend farmer's market suggested I try a couple of fennel bulbs—something I had never cooked with before. He's always encouraging me to experiment with new vegetables, and I trust his recommendations. I had never made anything with fennel bulb ever, so I decided to combine it with the sweet oranges from our backyard and see if I could create a salad. The combination of the crisp, slightly licorice-flavored fennel with sweet oranges and nutty Parmesan was so unexpectedly delicious that it's now one of my favorite salads.

For the Salad:

- 2 large fennel bulbs, trimmed and thinly sliced
- 3 navel oranges, peeled and segmented
- ⅓ cup pine nuts, toasted
- 2 oz Parmesan cheese, shaved with vegetable peeler
- ¼ cup fresh mint leaves
- 2 tablespoons fresh dill fronds
- Reserved fennel fronds for garnish

For the Citrus Vinaigrette:

- 2 tablespoons fresh orange juice with pulp
- 3 tablespoons extra-virgin olive oil
- 1 tablespoon fresh lemon juice
- 1 teaspoon orange zest
- ½ teaspoon sea salt
- ¼ teaspoon freshly ground black pepper
- Pinch of red pepper flakes (optional)
- Freshly cracked black pepper

Serves 4   Prep 20 mins   Cook 3 mins

PREPARE THE FENNEL: Trim the fennel bulbs. Use a mandoline or sharp knife to slice the fennel as thinly as possible, placing in ice water for 10 minutes to crisp up. Drain and dry the fennel slices and cut them into strips.

PREPARE THE ORANGES: Peel away all skin and white pith, then cut between membranes to create clean segments. (I was too lazy to do this, so I used the whole segments.)

MAKE THE VINAIGRETTE: Squeeze the juice from half an orange, including the pulp. Whisk together the olive oil, orange juice, lemon juice, orange zest, salt, pepper, and red pepper flakes until well emulsified and smooth.

TOAST THE PINE NUTS: Heat the pine nuts in a dry skillet over medium heat for 2-3 minutes until golden and fragrant, then allow them to cool completely.

ASSEMBLE THE SALAD: Arrange fennel strips and orange segments in a platter or bowl. Drizzle with vinaigrette. Scatter the shaved Parmesan, toasted pine nuts, mint leaves, and dill fronds, finishing with freshly cracked pepper.

Pair it with light Vermentino or Greco di Tufo, Aperol Spritz with fresh orange, or sparkling water with blood orange and fresh dill fronds.

Use a mandoline or very sharp knife to slice fennel paper-thin for the best texture and visual appeal. Save the fennel fronds as they add beautiful color and flavor as garnish. This salad is best served immediately after dressing to maintain the fennel's crispness.

ROOTS & LEAVES

GRILLED EGGPLANT ROLLS

In our first home, we had an Italian-American neighbor, Bernardi family, next door whose grandmother would visit from Italy. Whenever Nonna Carmelina came, they'd throw a neighborhood party and invite all the neighbors and friends. Since I loved cooking, I always volunteered to help her in the kitchen. She showed me how to slice eggplant paper-thin and grill it until it becomes pliable as silk. The key is getting those thin, even slices that char beautifully on the grill while staying flexible enough to roll. The smoky flavor from grilling adds depth that you just can't get any other way.

Serves 4   Prep 20 mins   Wait 20 mins   Grill/Cook 20 mins

- 2 large eggplants, sliced lengthwise into 1/4-inch strips
- 1 ½ teaspoon sea salt, divided
- ¼ cup olive oil, divided
- ½ teaspoon freshly ground black pepper, divided
- 1 small green bell pepper, diced
- 1 red onion, diced
- 2 cloves garlic, minced
- 1 small tomato, chopped
- 1 cup ricotta cheese
- ¼ cup pine nuts, toasted
- 2 tablespoons chopped fresh basil
- 1 tablespoon chopped fresh oregano
- 2 cups fresh arugula (optional)
- Balsamic glaze for drizzling (optional)

GRILL THE EGGPLANT: Rub the eggplant slices lightly with 1/2 teaspoon salt and let them sit for 20 minutes to draw out bitterness. Rinse under cold water and pat dry with paper towels. Brush the slices with 2 tablespoons of olive oil and season with 1/2 teaspoon salt and 1/4 teaspoon pepper. Grill on medium-high heat for 3-4 minutes per side until tender and charred with grill marks.

COOK THE VEGETABLES: Heat the remaining olive oil in a skillet over medium heat. Add the diced bell pepper and red onion. Cook them for 6-7 minutes until softened. Add the garlic and cook for 2 minutes until fragrant. Add chopped tomatoes and continue to cook for 2 minutes more.

MAKE THE FILLING: In a bowl, combine the ricotta cheese, cooked vegetables, toasted pine nuts, basil, oregano, 1/2 teaspoon salt, and ¼ teaspoon pepper. Mix everything well.

ASSEMBLE THE ROLLS: Place 2-3 tablespoons of filling at one end of each grilled eggplant slice. Roll tightly and secure with toothpicks if needed. Repeat the same for the rest of the slices.

GARNISH, DRIZZLE, AND SERVE: Arrange the rolls on serving plates, garnish with arugula if using and pine nuts. Drizzle with balsamic glaze if using before serving at room temperature.

Pair it with Chianti Classico or Barbera d'Alba, Italian chinotto with herbs, or sparkling water with blood orange and rosemary.

Don't overfill rolls or they'll unravel. When adding tomatoes to the skillet, keep the juice out to maintain the dry consistency of the filling. Make ahead, refrigerate up to four hours, and bring them to room temperature before serving.

BRAISED ARTICHOKE HEARTS WITH HERBS

I'll admit, prepping fresh artichokes used to intimidate me—all that trimming and removing tough leaves—but once you get the hang of it, it's actually quite meditative. The slow braising transforms the artichokes into something incredibly tender and flavorful, soaking up all the herbs and olive oil. It's become my favorite spring side dish, especially when artichokes are at their peak.

Serves 4   Prep 20 mins   Cook 25 mins

- 4 large fresh artichokes
- ½ cup fresh lemon juice, divided
- ⅓ cup extra virgin olive oil
- 1 medium red onion, chopped
- 4 cloves garlic, minced
- 2 tablespoons tomato paste
- ½ cup dry white wine
- 1 cup vegetable broth
- 3 sprigs fresh thyme
- ¼ cup chopped fresh flat-leaf parsley
- 2 tablespoons chopped fresh oregano
- 2 dried bay leaves
- 1 teaspoon sea salt
- ½ teaspoon freshly ground black pepper
- ¼ teaspoon red pepper flakes (optional)
- Extra herbs for garnish

PREPARE THE ARTICHOKES: Remove the tough outer leaves, trim the stems and tops, then scoop out the fuzzy chokes to reveal the hearts. Immediately place them in water with half the lemon juice to prevent browning.

BUILD THE AROMATIC BASE: Heat the olive oil in a large, heavy-bottomed skillet over medium heat. Add onion and cook for 4 minutes until softened. Add garlic and sauté for 2 minutes until fragrant.

SEAR THE ARTICHOKES: Increase the heat to medium-high. Add the artichoke hearts cut-side down to the skillet, cooking for 3-4 minutes until lightly golden. Add the tomato paste and cook for 1 minute more.

BRAISE UNTIL TENDER: Pour in the white wine, remaining lemon juice, vegetable broth, thyme sprigs, parsley, oregano, bay leaves, salt, pepper, and red pepper flakes if using. Bring it to a simmer.

FINISH AND SERVE: Cover and braise for 15-20 minutes until the artichokes are fork-tender. Remove the bay leaves, garnish with fresh herbs, and serve hot with the reduced braising liquid.

Pair it with Vermentino or Greco di Tufo white wine, Italian limoncello spritz, or sparkling water with lemon and rosemary.

When preparing artichokes, if they start browning, rub it with lemon. Don't overcook—artichoke hearts should be tender but not mushy. Save the braising liquid for drizzling over the finished dish.

GREEK POTATO GRATIN WITH KALAMATA OLIVES

This golden potato gratin became my way of combining the comfort of creamy layered potatoes with the bright flavors I love from Greek cooking. The key is scattering briny Kalamata olives throughout the creamy layers—they add bursts of salty complexity that transforms the whole dish. I also fold in fresh herbs and good olive oil, which gives the whole dish that Mediterranean warmth. It's perfect when I want a side that feels both familiar and a little unexpected.

Serves 4   Prep 15 mins   Cook/Bake 50 mins   Rest 10 mins

- 2 ½ tablespoons unsalted butter, divided
- 2 lbs Yukon Gold potatoes, peeled and sliced 1/8-inch thick
- ½ teaspoon sea salt
- ¼ teaspoon black pepper
- 2 tablespoons all-purpose flour
- 1 ½ cups whole milk, warmed
- ½ cup heavy cream
- 1 cup Gruyère cheese, grated
- ¼ cup Parmesan cheese, grated
- 2 cloves garlic, minced
- ⅛ teaspoon freshly grated nutmeg (a small pinch)
- 1 tablespoon chopped fresh oregano
- ½ cup Kalamata olives, pitted and halved
- 3 tablespoons fresh basil leaves

LAYER THE POTATOES: Preheat the oven to 375 °F (191 °C). Spread 1/2 tablespoon butter in a large cast-iron skillet or gratin dish. Arrange half the sliced potatoes in overlapping layers., Season with salt and pepper.

MAKE THE CHEESE SAUCE: Melt the butter in a saucepan over medium heat. Whisk in the flour and cook for 2 minutes. Gradually add the warm milk and cream, whisking constantly until smooth and thickened.

FINISH THE SAUCE: Remove the sauce from heat and stir in three-quarters of the Gruyère cheese, half the Parmesan, minced garlic, salt, pepper, nutmeg, and oregano until the cheese melts and the sauce is smooth.

ASSEMBLE THE GRATIN: Pour half the cheese sauce over the first layer of potatoes, scatter half the Kalamata olives on top. Repeat with the remaining potatoes, sauce, and olives, finishing with the remaining cheeses.

BAKE UNTIL GOLDEN: Cover with foil and bake for 30 minutes, then remove the foil and bake 15 minutes more until golden brown and bubbly. Let rest for 10 minutes before slicing. Garnish with fresh basil and serve hot.

Pair it with Assyrtiko or Santorini white wine, Greek mountain tea with honey, or sparkling water with fresh oregano and lemon.

Use a mandoline for uniform potato slices. Rinse potato slices to remove excess starch, then pat dry with paper towels before layering. Can be assembled ahead and baked when ready to serve.

STUFFED PORTOBELLO MUSHROOMS

These stuffed portobellos became my favorite dinner discovery when I was looking for creative ways to make vegetables the centerpiece of a meal. I was amazed at how naturally these large mushroom caps lend themselves to stuffing—their shape and size make them perfect vessels for all kinds of delicious fillings. The creamy ricotta and spinach filling transforms these earthy caps into something that feels substantial and elegant.

For the Mushrooms:
- 4 large portobello mushroom caps
- 2 tablespoons olive oil
- ½ teaspoon sea salt
- ¼ teaspoon freshly ground black pepper

For the Stuffing:
- 10 oz frozen spinach, thawed and thoroughly drained
- 1 cup whole milk ricotta cheese
- ½ cup freshly grated Parmesan cheese, divided
- ½ cup breadcrumbs, divided
- 2 cloves garlic, minced
- ⅛ teaspoon nutmeg
- ½ teaspoon dried Italian seasoning
- ¼ teaspoon red pepper flakes (optional)
- ¼ teaspoon sea salt
- ¼ teaspoon freshly ground black pepper

For Topping:
- 4-6 pieces vegan bacon, chopped (optional)
- Fresh basil leaves for garnish

Serves 4   Prep 15 mins   Bake 25 mins

PREPARE THE MUSHROOMS: Preheat the oven to 400 °F (204 °C). Clean the portobello caps by removing stems and scraping out dark gills with a spoon, creating clean bowl-shaped caps.

PRE-BAKE THE CAPS: Brush the mushroom caps inside and out with olive oil and season with salt and pepper. Place gill-side up on the parchment paper lined sheet pan and bake for 10 minutes to release moisture.

MAKE THE FILLING: Squeeze the thawed spinach in a clean kitchen towel to remove as much water as possible. Chop it roughly. Combine in a bowl with ricotta, 1/4 cup of Parmesan, 1/4 cup of breadcrumbs, garlic, nutmeg, Italian seasoning, red pepper flakes if using, salt, and pepper.

STUFF THE MUSHROOMS: Remove the partially baked mushrooms from the oven and pat dry the moisture. Divide the spinach-ricotta mixture evenly among the four caps, mounding it slightly in the center.

FINAL BAKE: Combine the remaining Parmesan cheese and breadcrumbs together and spread it over the top of the filling. Place the chopped vegan bacon if using on top. Return them to the oven for 12-15 minutes until the filling is heated through and the tops are golden brown.

GARNISH AND SERVE: Remove from the oven, garnish with fresh basil leaves and serve immediately while the filling is creamy and the mushrooms are tender.

Pair it with Italian Chianti or Sangiovese, Aperol Spritz with fresh herbs of your choice, or sparkling water with cucumber slices and fresh basil.

Squeeze spinach thoroughly—excess water will make the filling watery and prevent proper browning. Pre-baking mushrooms removes moisture and prevents soggy bottoms. These can be assembled ahead and refrigerated for up to four hours.

BAKED PASTA WITH EGGPLANT & TOMATOES

This hearty baked pasta became my answer to creating a satisfying vegetarian meal that feels indulgent without being heavy. The key is roasting the eggplant first until it's golden and tender, then combining it with pasta and a rich tomato sauce before baking everything together with plenty of cheese. What I love most is how the eggplant soaks up all the flavors while adding a meaty texture that makes this dish completely filling and comforting.

Serves 4   Prep 15 mins   Cook 18 mins   Roast/Bake 40 mins

- 2 medium eggplants, cut into 1-inch cubes
- 5 tablespoons olive oil, divided
- 1 teaspoon sea salt, divided
- ½ teaspoon freshly ground black pepper, divided
- 12 oz rigatoni or penne pasta
- 1 large onion, diced
- 4 cloves garlic, minced
- 2 tablespoons tomato paste
- 1 can (28 oz) crushed tomatoes
- 1 teaspoon dried oregano
- ½ teaspoon red pepper flakes (optional)
- ¼ cup chopped fresh basil
- 8 oz fresh mozzarella, torn into pieces
- ½ cup grated Parmesan cheese
- Store-bought pesto for drizzling (optional)
- Fresh basil leaves for garnish

ROAST THE EGGPLANT: Preheat the oven to 425 °F (218 °C). Toss cubed eggplant with 3 tablespoons olive oil, 1/2 teaspoon salt, and 1/4 teaspoon pepper. Spread on a large parchment paper lined sheet pan and roast for 20 minutes until golden brown and tender.

COOK THE PASTA: Meanwhile, bring a large pot of salted water to boil. Cook pasta according to package directions until just shy of al dente (it will finish cooking in the oven). Drain and set aside.

MAKE THE SAUCE: Heat remaining 2 tablespoons olive oil in a large skillet over medium heat. Add diced onion and cook for 5-6 minutes until softened. Add garlic and cook for 1 minute until fragrant. Stir in tomato paste and cook for 1 minute. Add crushed tomatoes, oregano, red pepper flakes if using, remaining 1/2 teaspoon salt, and 1/4 teaspoon pepper. Simmer for 10 minutes until slightly thickened.

ASSEMBLE: Reduce oven temperature to 375 °F (191 °C). In a large bowl, combine the cooked pasta, roasted eggplant, tomato sauce, and fresh basil. Transfer to a greased 9x13 inch baking dish. Top with torn mozzarella and grated Parmesan.

BAKE: Cover with foil and bake for 20 minutes. Remove foil and bake for an additional 10 minutes until cheese is golden and bubbly.

FINISH AND SERVE: Let it cool for 5 minutes. Drizzle with store-bought pesto if desired and garnish with fresh basil leaves before serving.

Pair it with Nero d'Avola or Chianti red wine, Italian chinotto with fresh basil, or sparkling water with blood orange and fresh oregano.

Can be assembled ahead and refrigerated before baking. Add 10 minutes to baking time if starting from cold.

ROASTED HEIRLOOM TOMATO GAZPACHO

While visiting Barcelona, a Spanish chef let me watch him cook for some time—Chef Xavier. I saw him roasting tomatoes first before adding them to a sauce. When I came back home, I tried applying that same technique to gazpacho. I was amazed by how the fire transformed the tomatoes—the caramelization concentrates all their natural sweetness into something much richer than traditional raw gazpacho. Combined with the classic bread, olive oil, and vinegar base, the roasted tomatoes create a soup that feels both familiar and completely new. This became my favorite way to use peak-season heirloom tomatoes.

For the Roasted Tomato Base:
- 3 pounds mixed heirloom tomatoes, cored and quartered
- 1 cup cherry tomatoes, halved
- 4 cloves garlic, peeled
- 1 medium red bell pepper, quartered
- 1 small red onion, quartered
- 3 tablespoons olive oil
- 1 teaspoon sea salt
- ½ teaspoon black pepper

For the Gazpacho:
- 1 thick slice day-old bread, crusts removed
- 2 tablespoons sherry vinegar
- 1 tablespoon balsamic vinegar
- ¼ cup extra-virgin olive oil
- 1 teaspoon sea salt
- ¼ teaspoon smoked paprika
- Pinch of cayenne pepper

For Garnish:
- Reserved roasted cherry tomatoes
- Fresh oregano and thyme
- Extra-virgin olive oil for drizzling
- Black pepper

Serves 4   Prep 15 mins   Roast 45 mins   Chill 2 hours

ROAST THE VEGETABLES: Preheat the oven to 425 °F (218 °C). On a large sheet pan lined with parchment paper, toss the heirloom tomatoes, cherry tomatoes, garlic cloves, bell pepper, and red onion with olive oil, salt, and pepper. Roast for 40-45 minutes until caramelized and charred.

PREPARE THE BREAD: Soak the bread slice in a bowl with enough water to cover for 5 minutes. Squeeze out the excess water and set aside the softened bread for blending.

CREATE THE GAZPACHO BASE: Remove the roasted vegetables from the oven. Reserve a few prettiest cherry tomatoes for garnish. Once the remaining roasted vegetables are cooled off, transfer them to a blender along with the soaked bread, sherry vinegar, and balsamic vinegar.

BLEND THE SOUP: Process until completely smooth. Slowly stream in the olive oil while blending. Season with salt, smoked paprika, and cayenne, and add cold water if needed to achieve the desired consistency.

CHILL AND SERVE: Transfer the gazpacho to the refrigerator for at least 2 hours until well chilled. Ladle the chilled soup into bowls. Garnish with the reserved roasted cherry tomatoes and fresh herb sprigs. Drizzle with olive oil and finish with cracked pepper.

Pair it with crisp Albariño or Verdejo, Spanish Manzanilla sherry, or sparkling water with thyme and a splash of sherry vinegar.

Gazpacho can be made up to two days ahead and refrigerated. Try fresh basil, parsley, or marjoram instead of oregano and thyme. To balance flavors, add more salt, vinegar, or a pinch of sugar.

ROOTS & LEAVES

LEBANESE GREEN BEANS IN TOMATO SAUCE

This beloved Lebanese dish became my introduction to the Middle Eastern tradition of slow-braising vegetables until they're meltingly tender and deeply flavorful. I discovered this recipe at a small Lebanese restaurant and was fascinated by the technique of cooking the beans long enough that they absorb every bit of the aromatic tomato sauce. What initially surprised me was serving it at room temperature, but I learned this allows all the flavors to meld beautifully, creating a dish that's both comforting and refreshing.

Serves 4 *Prep 15 mins* *Cook 30 mins*

- ¼ cup olive oil
- 1 medium onion, diced
- 3 cloves garlic, minced
- 1 tablespoon tomato paste
- 1 can (28 oz) crushed tomatoes
- 1 teaspoon sea salt
- ½ teaspoon freshly ground black pepper
- ½ teaspoon ground allspice
- ¼ teaspoon ground cinnamon
- 1 ½ lbs fresh green beans, trimmed and cut into 2 to 3 inch pieces
- 1 cup vegetable broth
- ¼ cup chopped fresh flat-leaf parsley
- 1 tablespoons chopped fresh mint
- ½ tablespoon lemon juice
- Extra herbs for garnish

BUILD THE AROMATIC BASE: Heat the olive oil in a large, heavy-bottomed pot over medium heat. Add the diced onion and cook for 6-7 minutes until softened and lightly golden.

ADD THE AROMATICS: Add the minced garlic and cook for 1-2 minutes until fragrant. Stir in the tomato paste and cook for another minute until darkened.

CREATE THE SAUCE: Add the crushed tomatoes, salt, pepper, allspice, and cinnamon to the pot, stirring to combine. Bring it to a gentle simmer.

BRAISE THE BEANS: Add the green beans and vegetable broth to the pot and bring to a boil. Reduce heat to low, cover, and simmer for 20 minutes or until the beans are very tender and the sauce has thickened.

FINISH AND COOL: Remove from heat and stir in the fresh parsley, mint, and lemon juice. Let it cool to room temperature before serving, garnished with extra herbs.

Pair it with Lebanese Château Ksara red wine, Arabic coffee with cardamom, or fresh mint tea with honey and orange blossom water.

Sautéing the tomato paste in oil deepens its flavor. Don't undercook the beans—they should be very tender, not crisp. Let the dish cool to room temperature for best flavor.

ROASTED CAULIFLOWER WITH CHERMOULA

Roasting cauliflower until it's golden and caramelized completely changed how I think about this vegetable. The real game-changer, though, is the chermoula—a Moroccan herb sauce packed with cilantro, parsley, and warm spices that I learned about while exploring North African cooking. The bright, fresh sauce against the sweet, nutty roasted cauliflower is one of those combinations that just works, turning an everyday vegetable into something you actually crave.

Serves 4   Prep 20 mins   Roast 20 mins

For the Cauliflower:
- 1 large head cauliflower
- 3 tablespoons olive oil
- 1 teaspoon ground cumin
- 1 teaspoon smoked paprika
- ½ teaspoon ground coriander
- ½ teaspoon turmeric
- 1 teaspoon sea salt
- ½ teaspoon black pepper

For the Chermoula:
- 1 cup chopped fresh cilantro
- ½ cup chopped fresh flat-leaf parsley
- 3 cloves garlic, minced
- ¼ cup extra virgin olive oil
- 2 tablespoons lemon juice
- 1 tablespoon lemon zest
- 1 teaspoon ground cumin
- ½ teaspoon sweet paprika
- ¼ teaspoon cayenne pepper
- ½ teaspoon sea salt

For Serving:
- 1 cup Greek yogurt, beaten
- Fresh cilantro leaves for garnish

PREPARE THE CAULIFLOWER: Preheat the oven to 450 °F (232 °C). Cut the cauliflower into 4 thick steaks from the center. If you can't get 4 steaks from your cauliflower, break the remaining head into large, substantial florets that will caramelize properly.

SEASON AND ROAST: In a small bowl, combine olive oil, cumin, smoked paprika, coriander, turmeric, salt, and pepper. Drizzle this spice oil over the cauliflower, rubbing it in with your fingers until evenly coated. Arrange the cauliflower steaks in a single layer on a large sheet pan lined with parchment paper.

ROAST UNTIL GOLDEN: Roast for 18-20 minutes, flipping halfway through, until the cauliflower is golden brown and caramelized on the edges while remaining tender in the center with beautiful char marks.

MAKE THE CHERMOULA: Combine the cilantro, parsley, minced garlic, olive oil, lemon juice, lemon zest, cumin, paprika, cayenne, and salt in a bowl, whisking until well combined and vibrant green.

ASSEMBLE THE DISH: Spread the Greek yogurt on a serving platter. Arrange the roasted cauliflower over the yogurt. Drizzle generously with the chermoula sauce, allowing some to pool on the yogurt base.

GARNISH AND SERVE: Garnish with fresh cilantro leaves. Serve immediately while the cauliflower is hot and the chermoula is aromatic.

Pair it with Moroccan red wine or Côtes du Rhône, fresh mint tea with honey, or sparkling water with orange blossom and parsley.

Cut cauliflower into substantial pieces to prevent overcooking and ensure proper caramelization. Chermoula can be made up to 2 days ahead and refrigerated. For deeper flavor, marinate cauliflower in spice mixture for thirty minutes before roasting.

ARUGULA SALAD WITH PEARS & BLUE CHEESE

This elegant salad holds a special place in my heart because of the sweet pears that used to come from our backyard tree. Over the years, our pear tree naturally grafted with the neighboring apple tree, creating an entirely different fruit—one of those amazing miracles of nature. I miss those original sweet pears terribly, and this salad was one of my favorite ways to showcase them at their peak. Now when I make it with store-bought pears, I'm always transported back to those days when the peppery arugula, tangy blue cheese, and toasted walnuts created the perfect stage for my homegrown pears to truly shine.

For the Vinaigrette:
- 3 tablespoons extra-virgin olive oil
- 2 tablespoons balsamic vinegar
- 1 tablespoon honey
- 1 teaspoon Dijon mustard
- ½ teaspoon sea salt
- ¼ teaspoon freshly ground black pepper

For the Salad:
- 2 ripe pears (Anjou or Bartlett)
- 1 tablespoon lemon juice
- ½ cup walnuts
- 6 cups fresh arugula, washed and patted dry
- 4 oz blue cheese, crumbled
- Freshly cracked black pepper

Serves 4   Prep 15 mins   Cook 3 mins

PREPARE THE VINAIGRETTE: Whisk together the olive oil, balsamic vinegar, honey, Dijon mustard, salt, and pepper in a small bowl until well emulsified and smooth. Set aside to let the flavors meld.

PREPARE THE PEARS: Core and slice the pears into thin wedges. Immediately toss with fresh lemon juice to prevent browning and maintain their beautiful color.

TOAST THE WALNUTS: Heat the walnuts in a dry skillet over medium heat for 2-3 minutes until fragrant and lightly golden. Allow them to cool completely before roughly chopping.

ASSEMBLE THE SALAD: Place the arugula in a large serving bowl. Arrange the pear slices throughout the greens. Scatter the crumbled blue cheese and toasted walnuts evenly over the surface.

FINISH AND SERVE: Drizzle the honey balsamic vinaigrette over the salad and gently toss to coat all ingredients. Garnish with freshly cracked black pepper before serving immediately.

Pair it with light Chardonnay or Viognier, sparkling apple cider with herbs of your choice, or elderflower sparkling water with fresh pear slices.

Choose pears that are ripe but still firm to prevent them from becoming mushy when tossed with dressing. Toast walnuts just before serving for maximum crunch and flavor.

ZUCCHINI PASTA WITH BASIL PESTO & BURRATA

When our neighbor's prolific zucchini plants started producing more than they could handle, I found myself with bags of fresh zucchini and a mission to use them creatively. This dish became my favorite way to turn that abundance into something special—spiralized zucchini tossed with homemade basil pesto and topped with creamy burrata. It's light enough for hot summer days but feels indulgent enough to serve to guests, and I love making extra to share back with the same neighbor who keeps us supplied with zucchini. The combination of fresh herbs, good olive oil, and that luxurious burrata makes simple zucchini feel like a celebration.

Serves 4   Prep 20 mins   Cook 3 mins

For the Zucchini Pasta:
- 4 large zucchini
- 2 tablespoons olive oil
- ½ teaspoon sea salt
- ¼ teaspoon black pepper

For the Basil Pesto:
- 2 cups fresh basil leaves, packed
- ⅓ cup pine nuts, toasted
- 3 cloves garlic, minced
- ½ cup grated Parmesan cheese
- ¼ teaspoon sea salt
- ¼ teaspoon black pepper
- ½ cup extra virgin olive oil

For Assembly:
- 8 oz fresh burrata cheese
- Extra basil leaves for garnish
- Red pepper flakes (optional)

SPIRALIZE THE ZUCCHINI: Use an electric or handheld spiralizer to create zucchini noodles. Place the zucchini pasta on a paper towel or kitchen towel and squeeze it lightly to remove the excess moisture.

COOK THE ZUCCHINI PASTA: Heat the olive oil in a large skillet over high heat. Add the spiralized zucchini and sauté for 2-3 minutes until just tender but still al dente, seasoning with salt and pepper.

MAKE THE PESTO: Combine the basil leaves, toasted pine nuts, garlic, Parmesan, salt, and pepper in a food processor. Pulse to chop and combine. With the food processor running, slowly drizzle in the olive oil until smooth pesto is formed.

TOSS WITH PESTO: Remove the skillet from heat and immediately toss the warm zucchini pasta with the prepared pesto until evenly coated and vibrant green.

PLATE THE DISH: Divide the pesto-coated zucchini pasta among serving plates, creating neat nests or mounds for elegant presentation.

ADD THE BURRATA: Top each serving with torn burrata cheese. Garnish with fresh basil leaves and red pepper flakes if using. Serve immediately while the zucchini pasta is still warm.

Pair it with Pinot Grigio or Vermentino white wine, Italian limonata, or sparkling water with lemon and fresh basil.

Don't overcook zucchini noodles to maintain texture. Make pesto fresh for the best flavor. Tear burrata just before serving to prevent it from becoming watery. If you don't have a spiralizer, use a vegetable peeler to make long strips, then cut them into ribbons.

TUSCAN RIBOLLITA SOUP WITH BREAD

This simple pasta became my lesson in how Mediterranean cooks turn basic pantry staples into something completely satisfying and delicious. I discovered that the magic happens when pasta water combines with olive oil and garlic to create a silky sauce, while fresh lemon adds brightness that transforms everything. It embodies everything I love about this style of cooking: honoring tradition, using what you have on hand, and finding joy in simple, everyday ingredients.

Serves 4 Prep 20 mins Cook 50 mins Rest 5 mins

- 3 tablespoons olive oil
- 1 medium onion, diced
- 1 medium potato, cubed
- 2 carrots, diced
- 2 celery stalks, diced
- 3 cloves garlic, minced
- 1 can (about 14.5 oz) diced tomatoes
- 4 cups vegetable broth
- 1 can (about 15 oz) cannellini beans, drained and rinsed
- 3 cups torn chunks of a day-old Italian bread
- 3 cups chopped fresh spinach
- 1½ cups chopped baby kale
- 3 tablespoons chopped basil
- 1½ tablespoons chopped fresh rosemary
- 1½ teaspoons sea salt
- ½ teaspoon black pepper
- ½ cup shredded Parmesan cheese, plus for serving
- Extra fresh herbs for garnish
- 1 tablespoon extra virgin olive oil for drizzling

BUILD THE VEGETABLE BASE: Heat the olive oil in a large, heavy-bottomed pot over medium heat. Add the diced onion, potatoes, carrots, and celery. Cook for 8-10 minutes until the vegetables soften and begin to caramelize.

ADD AROMATICS: Add the minced garlic and cook for 1-2 minutes until fragrant. Stir in the diced tomatoes and cook for 5 minutes until the tomatoes break down slightly.

CREATE THE SOUP BASE: Add the vegetable broth, cannellini beans, and torn bread chunks to the pot. Bring it to a boil. Cover the pot and reduce heat to simmer for 20-25 minutes until the bread breaks down and the soup thickens. Be sure to stir in between a few times.

ADD THE GREENS AND HERBS: Stir in the chopped spinach, kale, fresh basil, rosemary, salt, and pepper. Cook for 5-8 minutes more until the greens are wilted and tender.

FINISH AND SERVE: Remove from heat and stir in the Parmesan cheese. Ladle into bowls and serve hot with extra cheese, fresh herbs, and a drizzle of extra virgin olive oil.

Pair it with Chianti Classico or Sangiovese, Italian espresso with a touch of sugar, or sparkling water with fresh sage and lemon.

Let the soup rest for 5 minutes for the flavors to develop. Serve hot with thin toasted slices of Italian bread. Ribollita tastes even better the next day when reheated.

EGGPLANT PARMESAN ON GARLIC BREAD

This innovative take on eggplant parmigiana came about when I was craving the classic Italian dish but wanted something more substantial and satisfying than the traditional version. I had some leftover garlic bread and decided to use it as the foundation, which turned out to be a great idea. The crispy garlic bread base elevates the tender, cheesy eggplant into an indulgent open-faced sandwich that's become one of my favorite comfort food creations.

Serves 4   Prep 15 mins   Wait 30 mins   Cook/Bake 25 mins

For the Eggplant:
- 1 large eggplant, sliced into 1/2-inch rounds
- 1 teaspoon sea salt
- ½ cup all-purpose flour
- 1 large egg, beaten
- 1 cup Italian breadcrumbs
- ⅓ cup olive oil for frying

For the Garlic Bread:
- 1/3 cup unsalted butter, softened
- 3 cloves garlic, minced
- 3 tablespoons chopped fresh flat-leaf parsley
- 3 tablespoons grated Parmesan cheese
- ¼ teaspoon sea salt
- 4 thick slices Italian bread or ciabatta

For Assembly:
- 1 cup marinara sauce
- 4 slices of fresh mozzarella
- ⅓ cup Parmesan cheese, grated
- Fresh basil leaves for garnish

PREPARE THE EGGPLANT: Slice the eggplant into rounds. Salt generously and let them drain in a colander for 30 minutes to remove bitterness and extra moisture. Pat them dry completely with paper towels.

BREAD THE EGGPLANT: Set up a breading station with flour, beaten egg, and breadcrumbs in separate shallow dishes. Coat each eggplant slice in flour, egg, and breadcrumbs, pressing gently to adhere. Use one hand for wet ingredients (egg) and the other for dry ingredients (flour and breadcrumbs) to prevent clumping on your fingers.

FRY THE EGGPLANT: Heat the olive oil in a large skillet over medium-high heat. Fry the breaded eggplant slices in batches for 3-4 minutes per side until golden brown and cooked through. Drain them on paper towels.

MAKE THE GARLIC BREAD: Combine the softened butter with minced garlic, parsley, Parmesan, and salt. Spread it evenly on the bread slices and toast under the broiler until golden and fragrant, about 3 minutes.

ASSEMBLE AND BAKE: Preheat the oven to 425 °F (218 °C). Place the garlic bread on a parchment paper lined sheet pan. Spread half the marinara sauce over the garlic bread. Then start layering with fried eggplant, mozzarella slices, remaining marinara sauce, and grated Parmesan.

FINISH AND SERVE: Bake for 12-14 minutes until the cheese is melted and bubbly. Garnish with fresh basil leaves before serving hot.

Pair it with Chianti Classico or Barbera d'Alba, Italian chinotto soda with fresh basil, or sparkling water with lemon and fresh oregano.

Salt eggplant slices and drain thoroughly to remove bitterness and prevent soggy texture. Toast garlic bread just until golden to prevent burning during final baking. Use fresh mozzarella for best melting quality.

PASTA SALAD WITH ROASTED VEGETABLES

I used to think pasta salad was just a boring picnic side dish until I started roasting the vegetables first. The high heat caramelizes everything—peppers get sweet and slightly charred, zucchini becomes tender, and even mushrooms develop this amazing depth. When served at room temperature, all the flavors meld beautifully, making it perfect for gatherings and potlucks. I've brought this to several community events, and it's become one of those dishes that always gets compliments and requests for the recipe.

Serves 4   Prep 25 mins   Cook 10 mins   Roast 20 mins

- 1 large red bell pepper, cut into bite-sized pieces
- 1 large yellow bell pepper, cut into bite-sized pieces
- 1 large zucchini, sliced into half-moons
- 8 oz cremini mushrooms, quartered
- 1 cup cherry tomatoes, halved
- ½ cup olive oil, divided
- 1 teaspoon sea salt
- ½ teaspoon black pepper
- 12 oz farfalle (bow-tie) pasta
- 2 tablespoons balsamic vinegar
- 1 clove garlic, minced
- ½ cup Kalamata olives, pitted and halved
- 2 tablespoons chopped basil
- 2 tablespoons chopped fresh curly-leaf parsley
- 1 tablespoons chopped fresh oregano
- ½ cup grated Parmesan cheese
- Extra herbs for garnish

ROAST THE VEGETABLES: Preheat the oven to 425 °F (218 °C). Toss the bell peppers, zucchini, mushrooms, and cherry tomatoes with ¼ cup olive oil, ½ teaspoon salt, and ¼ teaspoon pepper. Spread the vegetables on a parchment paper lined large sheet pan. Roast for 20 minutes or until the vegetables are caramelized and tender.

COOK THE PASTA: Cook the pasta according to package directions until al dente, usually 8 to 10 minutes. Drain and rinse with cold water to stop cooking. Transfer to a large serving bowl.

MAKE THE DRESSING: Whisk together the remaining olive oil, balsamic vinegar, minced garlic, remaining ½ teaspoon salt, and ¼ teaspoon pepper in a small bowl to create the dressing.

COMBINE EVERYTHING: Add the roasted vegetables, Kalamata olives, fresh basil, parsley, oregano, and dressing to the cooled pasta. Toss gently to combine all ingredients.

FINISH AND SERVE: Sprinkle with the grated Parmesan cheese, garnish with extra fresh herbs, and serve at room temperature or chilled.

Pair it with Pinot Grigio or Vermentino white wine, Italian limonata with fresh herbs, or sparkling water with cucumber and fresh basil.

Don't overcook pasta as it will continue to soften in the salad. Let vegetables cool slightly before mixing. Salad tastes best when flavors have time to meld for at least thirty minutes.

Fire & Feast
Hearty Mediterranean Meat Dishes

STUFFED EGGPLANT WITH SPICED CHICKEN

This elegant dish transformed how I think about eggplant—turning it into edible vessels that cradle aromatic spiced chicken rather than just serving it as a side. The secret is roasting the eggplant until it becomes silky and almost custard-like, creating the perfect foundation for bold flavors. The cooling yogurt sauce provides the ideal contrast to the warm spices, embodying the Mediterranean principle of balancing rich and refreshing elements in every bite. It's become one of my favorite ways to make a meal that feels both exotic and comforting.

Serves 4   Prep 25 mins   Roast 40 mins

For the Eggplant:

- 2 large eggplants, halved lengthwise
- 3 tablespoons olive oil
- 1 teaspoon sea salt

For the Spiced Chicken:

- 1 lb boneless skinless chicken breast
- 2 tablespoons olive oil
- 1 teaspoon ground cumin
- 1 teaspoon smoked paprika
- ½ teaspoon ground coriander
- ½ teaspoon dried oregano
- ½ teaspoon sea salt
- ¼ teaspoon black pepper
- 2 cups fresh baby spinach
- ¼ cup chopped flat-leaf parsley

For the Yogurt-Cheese Sauce:

- 1 cup Greek yogurt
- ¼ cup ricotta cheese
- 2 tablespoons lemon juice
- 1 clove garlic, minced
- 2 tablespoons finely diced red onion
- 2 tablespoons chopped basil
- ¼ teaspoon sea salt
- Extra spinach, herbs, and red onion for garnish

ROAST THE EGGPLANT: Preheat the oven to 425 °F (218 °C). Score the eggplant flesh in a crosshatch pattern. Brush the scored eggplants with olive oil and salt. Roast cut-side down on a large parchment paper lined sheet pan for 35-40 minutes until completely tender.

COOK THE CHICKEN: Pat dry the chicken breasts with a paper towel and cut them into bite-sized pieces. Toss them with olive oil, cumin, paprika, coriander, oregano, salt, and pepper. Spread on a separate parchment paper lined sheet pan and roast for 20-25 minutes until golden and cooked through. Both eggplant and chicken can roast simultaneously in the oven.

MAKE THE SAUCE: While the chicken and eggplant cook, whisk together the Greek yogurt, ricotta cheese, lemon juice, minced garlic, red onion, basil, and salt until smooth and creamy.

COMBINE THE FILLING: Remove the cooked chicken from the oven and immediately toss with the fresh baby spinach and parsley, allowing the heat to wilt the greens.

ASSEMBLE AND SERVE: Remove the roasted eggplants from the oven and flip them over with cut-side up. Top generously with the chicken-spinach filling. Spoon the yogurt-cheese sauce over everything and garnish with extra spinach, herbs, and chopped red onion before serving.

Pair it with Côtes du Rhône or Lebanese red wine, Turkish coffee with cardamom, or pomegranate juice with mint & sparkling water.

Don't skip scoring the eggplant flesh—it ensures even cooking and better flavor absorption. Toss the baby spinach with hot chicken to wilt it perfectly. The yogurt sauce can be made a day ahead and refrigerated, but add the chopped onion just before serving.

GRILLED LEMON PESTO CHICKEN

This vibrant grilled chicken has become one of my family's most requested Mediterranean dinners. The combination of lemon, olive oil, and fresh herbs in the marinade makes the chicken incredibly flavorful and tender, while grilling gives it those perfect charred edges. What really makes this special is the fresh herb pesto —I spoon it generously over the grilled chicken and serve extra on the side. It adds this bright, punchy flavor that transforms the whole dish.

For the Chicken:
- ¼ cup olive oil
- 3 cloves garlic, minced
- 2 tablespoons lemon juice
- 1 tablespoon lemon zest
- 2 teaspoons dried oregano
- 1 teaspoon sea salt
- ½ teaspoon black pepper
- 4 boneless, skinless chicken breasts (6 oz each)

For the Herb Pesto:
- 2 cups packed basil leaves
- ¼ cup fresh flat-leaf parsley
- ¼ cup pine nuts, toasted
- 2 cloves garlic
- ½ cup olive oil
- ¼ cup grated Parmesan cheese
- ¼ teaspoon sea salt
- ¼ teaspoon black pepper

For Grilling:
- Extra olive oil for brushing
- 2 lemons, halved
- 1 large beefsteak tomato, sliced 1/4-inch slices

Serves 4   Prep 15 mins   Wait 30 mins   Grill 20 mins

MARINATE THE CHICKEN: In a large bowl, combine the olive oil, minced garlic, lemon juice, lemon zest, oregano, salt, and pepper. Add the chicken breasts and toss to coat with the marinade. Marinate for 30 minutes to 2 hours refrigerated.

MAKE THE PESTO: Combine the basil, parsley, toasted pine nuts, and garlic in a food processor. Pulse until chopped. Slowly add the olive oil while processing until smooth. Finally stir in the Parmesan, salt, and pepper.

PREPARE FOR GRILLING: Preheat the grill or grill pan to medium-high heat and brush the grates with oil to prevent sticking.

GRILL THE CHICKEN: Remove the chicken from the marinade and grill for 8-10 minutes per side until the internal temperature reaches 165 °F (74 °C) and beautiful grill marks form.

GRILL THE VEGETABLES: Brush the tomato slices with olive oil. During the last few minutes of cooking, add the lemon halves and tomato slices to the grill. Cook until lightly charred and caramelized.

GARNISH AND SERVE: Let the chicken rest for a few minutes before serving. Serve topped with fresh pesto alongside the grilled lemons and tomato slices. Drizzle any remaining pesto around the plate.

Pair it with Vermentino or Falanghina white wine, Italian Aperol spritz with basil, or sparkling water with elderflower and lemon.

Marinate chicken for at least 30 minutes but no more than 4 hours to prevent texture changes. Use a meat thermometer to ensure chicken reaches safe internal temperature without overcooking. Pesto can be made up to three days ahead and refrigerated.

TURKEY MEATBALLS IN HERB CREAM SAUCE

I developed this recipe when I wanted all the comfort of traditional meatballs but with a lighter, more Mediterranean twist. Using turkey instead of beef keeps them tender, and the herb-packed cream sauce with fresh spinach makes every bite feel indulgent without being heavy. What surprised me the first time I made this was how quickly it comes together—once the meatballs are browned and cooked through, they get nestled into this creamy sauce where all the flavors meld beautifully.

For the Turkey Meatballs:

- 1 ½ lbs ground turkey
- ½ cup Italian breadcrumbs
- ¼ cup grated Parmesan cheese
- 1 large egg, beaten
- 3 cloves garlic, minced
- 2 tablespoons chopped fresh flat-leaf parsley
- 1 teaspoon sea salt
- ½ teaspoon black pepper
- 2 tablespoons olive oil for cooking

For the Creamy Spinach Sauce:

- 2 tablespoons butter
- 1 medium onion, diced
- 4 cloves garlic, minced
- 1 cup heavy cream
- ½ cup chicken broth
- 5 oz fresh baby spinach
- ¼ cup grated Parmesan cheese
- ½ teaspoon sea salt
- ¼ teaspoon black pepper
- ⅛ teaspoon nutmeg
- Red pepper flakes for garnish (optional)

Serves 4   Prep 20 mins   Cook 25 mins

MAKE THE MEATBALLS: Combine the ground turkey, Italian breadcrumbs, Parmesan, beaten egg, garlic, parsley, salt, and pepper in a bowl. Mix it gently until just combined. Form into 16-18 meatballs.

BROWN THE MEATBALLS: Heat the olive oil in a large skillet over medium-high heat. Brown the meatballs on all sides for 10 minutes until browned and the internal temperature reaches 165 °F (74 °C). Remove and set aside.

START THE SAUCE: In the same skillet, melt the butter on medium heat. Sauté the diced onion for 4-5 minutes until softened. Add the garlic and cook for 1-2 minutes until fragrant.

FINISH THE SAUCE: Pour in the heavy cream and chicken broth, bringing to a gentle simmer. Add the fresh baby spinach in batches, stirring until wilted and incorporated. Stir in the Parmesan cheese, salt, pepper, and nutmeg. Cook for 2-3 minutes until the sauce thickens slightly and the cheese melts completely.

COMBINE AND SERVE: Return the meatballs to the skillet, nestling them in the creamy spinach sauce. Simmer for 3-4 minutes to heat through. Garnish with red pepper flakes if using before serving.

Pair it with Chianti Classico or Sangiovese red wine, Italian Prosecco with fresh parsley, or sparkling water with lemon and fresh rosemary.

Don't overmix the meatball mixture to keep them tender—mix just until ingredients are combined. Use a gentle touch when forming meatballs for the best texture. Sauce can be made ahead and reheated gently.

GREEK LEMON RICE SOUP WITH CHICKEN

This soul-warming Greek soup became my masterclass in the ancient technique of avgolemono (sounds like av·gow·luh·maa·now). It's this magical egg-lemon combination that transforms simple broth into silky, luxurious comfort. The secret lies in the tempering process: slowly whisking hot broth into beaten eggs to create that signature velvety texture without scrambling. The bright, tangy lemon that permeates every spoonful represents the heart of Greek home cooking—simple ingredients elevated through time-honored methods and genuine care.

Serves 6   Prep 15 mins   Cook 45 mins

- 2 tablespoons olive oil
- 1 medium onion, diced
- 2 large carrots, diced
- 2 celery stalks, diced
- 3 cloves garlic, minced
- 8 cups chicken broth
- 1 lb boneless, skinless chicken breast
- ¾ cup long-grain white rice
- 2 large eggs
- 4 tablespoons lemon juice
- 1 tablespoon lemon zest
- 1 teaspoon sea salt
- ½ teaspoon black pepper
- ¼ teaspoon dried oregano
- 4 tablespoons chopped fresh flat-leaf parsley
- 2 tablespoons chopped dill
- Thin lemon slices for garnish
- Extra herbs for garnish

BUILD THE BASE: Heat the olive oil in a large pot over medium heat. Add the diced onion, carrots, and celery, cooking for 5-6 minutes until softened. Add the garlic and cook for 2 minutes until fragrant.

COOK THE CHICKEN: Add the chicken broth and chicken breasts to the pot and bring to a boil. Reduce heat to medium-low and simmer for 15-20 minutes until the chicken is cooked through and tender. Remove the chicken from the pot and shred into bite-sized pieces.

ADD THE RICE: Add the rice to the pot and simmer for 15-18 minutes until the rice is tender. Add the shredded chicken back to the pot.

PREPARE THE AVGOLEMONO: In a medium bowl, whisk the eggs. Stir in lemon juice and lemon zest until well combined. Slowly add ½ cup of hot broth while whisking constantly to temper the eggs. Be sure to add the hot broth gradually to prevent the eggs from scrambling.

FINISH THE SOUP: Remove the soup from heat and slowly stir in the egg-lemon mixture while stirring constantly. Season with salt, pepper, oregano, fresh parsley, and dill. Garnish with lemon slices and herbs before serving hot.

Pair it with Assyrtiko or Santorini white wine, Greek mountain tea with honey, or sparkling water with lemon and fresh oregano.

Temper eggs slowly to prevent curdling—patience is key for the perfect texture. Stir constantly when adding the egg-lemon mixture for smooth consistency. Don't heat the soup after adding the egg mixture.

HERB-CRUSTED LAMB CHOPS

I used to be intimidated by cooking lamb until I learned how simple it really is when you don't overthink it. The key is creating a fragrant herb crust that caramelizes beautifully on the outside while keeping the meat tender and juicy inside. The cooling yogurt sauce provides the perfect tangy contrast to the rich lamb and aromatic herbs. What I love about this dish is how it looks and tastes elegant but comes together quickly once you have everything prepped.

For the Lamb Chops:
- 3 tablespoons olive oil
- 3 cloves garlic, minced
- 2 tablespoons minced fresh rosemary
- 1 tablespoon minced fresh thyme
- 1 tablespoon minced fresh oregano
- 1 teaspoon sea salt
- ½ teaspoon black pepper
- ¼ teaspoon smoked paprika
- 8 lamb rib chops, frenched

For the Yogurt Sauce:
- 1 cup Greek yogurt
- 2 tablespoons chopped fresh mint
- 1 tablespoon chopped fresh dill
- 1 clove garlic, minced
- 1 tablespoon lemon juice
- ½ teaspoon sea salt
- ¼ teaspoon white pepper

For Serving:
- Lemon wedges
- Fresh herb sprigs for garnish

Serves 4   Prep 25 mins   Broil 10-14 mins   Rest 5 mins

MARINATE THE LAMB: Combine the olive oil, minced garlic, rosemary, thyme, oregano, salt, pepper, and paprika in a bowl. Rub this mixture all over the lamb chops and let marinate at room temperature for 20 minutes or until the meat comes to room temperature before cooking.

MAKE THE YOGURT SAUCE: While the lamb marinates, whisk together the Greek yogurt, mint, dill, garlic, lemon juice, salt, and white pepper until smooth and well combined. Refrigerate it until serving.

PREPARE FOR BROILING: Position the oven rack 6 inches from the broiler element. Set the oven setting and temperature to "Broil" and preheat the oven. Line a sheet pan with foil for easy cleanup.

BROIL THE CHOPS: Arrange the marinated lamb chops on the prepared sheet pan. Broil until a beautiful golden-brown crust is formed.

USE MEAT THERMOMETER: Broil for 4-5 minutes per side for medium-rare (140 °F/60 °C), 5-6 minutes per side for medium (150 °F/66 °C), or 6-7 minutes per side for medium-well (160 °F/71 °C). These times are for 1-inch thick chops.

REST AND SERVE: Let the lamb chops rest for 5 minutes before serving with the yogurt sauce, fresh lemon wedges, and herb sprigs for garnish.

Pair it with Côtes du Rhône or Greek Nemea red wine, Greek mountain tea with honey, or sparkling water with lime & rosemary.

Ask your butcher to french the chops, which means removing the meat and fat from the rib bones for a more elegant presentation. Use a meat thermometer for perfect doneness every time.

MEDITERRANEAN GRAIN & CHICKEN BOWL

This vibrant bowl became my answer to creating satisfying, nourishing meals that celebrate the Mediterranean tradition of balancing grains, proteins, and fresh vegetables in perfect harmony. I discovered freekeh during my exploration of ancient grains, learning how this nutty, smoky wheat provides the ideal foundation for building colorful, textured bowls. The quick pickled onions add a bright acidic pop that is essential for tying together rich and fresh elements, creating a meal that's as beautiful as it is satisfying.

Serves 4   Prep 25 mins   Cook 35 mins   Rest 5 mins

For the Chicken:

- 2 boneless, skinless chicken breasts
- 2 tablespoons olive oil
- 2 teaspoons dried oregano
- 1 teaspoon garlic powder
- ½ teaspoon sea salt
- ¼ teaspoon black pepper

For the Quick Pickled Onions:

- ½ cup apple cider vinegar
- 2 tablespoons water
- 1 tablespoon sugar
- ½ teaspoon sea salt
- 1 small red onion, sliced

For the Bowl:

- 2 cups freekeh/bulgur wheat
- 1 large orange bell pepper, cut into strips
- 1 teaspoon olive oil
- 2 cups fresh spinach
- 1 can (15 oz) fava beans, drained and rinsed
- 1 cup cherry tomatoes, halved
- 1 cucumber, sliced
- ½ cup crumbled feta cheese
- ¼ cup Greek yogurt (optional)
- 1 tablespoon lemon juice

PREPARE THE CHICKEN: Season the chicken breasts with olive oil, oregano, garlic powder, salt, and pepper. Marinate for 20 minutes.

MAKE THE PICKLED ONIONS: While the chicken is marinating, combine the vinegar, water, sugar, and salt in a bowl. Add the sliced onions and let sit for 20 minutes while preparing other components.

COOK THE GRAINS: Cook the freekeh according to package directions until tender, about 20-25 minutes. Drain and set aside to cool slightly.

COOK THE CHICKEN: Pan-sear the chicken breasts at medium-high heat for 6-7 minutes per side until cooked through and the internal temperature reaches 165 °F (74 °C). Let the chicken rest for 5 minutes.

COOK BELL PEPPERS: While the chicken rests, return the same pan to medium-high heat. Add olive oil and quickly sauté the bell pepper strips for 2 minutes until tender, but not soft.

ASSEMBLE AND SERVE: Slice the chicken into strips. Assemble bowls with cooked freekeh, spinach, fava beans, bell peppers, cherry tomatoes, cucumber, and feta cheese. Top each bowl with sliced chicken, drained pickled onions, and a dollop of Greek yogurt if using. Drizzle with the lemon juice before serving.

Pair it with Sauvignon Blanc or Vermentino white wine, Greek Freddo cappuccino, or sparkling water with tangerine and mint.

Pickled onions can be made up to three days ahead and stored refrigerated. Let chicken rest before slicing for the juiciest results. Assemble bowls just before serving to maintain optimal texture contrast.

STUFFED PORK TENDERLOIN WITH HERBS & FETA

I used to think stuffed meats were too complicated until I made this pork tenderloin. The "butterfly" technique looked intimidating at first, but once I learned how to do it, it's actually quite straightforward. The fresh Mediterranean herbs and creamy feta create these beautiful spirals when you slice the meat, making it look much fancier than the effort it takes. What I love most is how the herbs and cheese keep the pork incredibly moist and flavorful.

Serves 6   Prep 30 mins   Cook/Roast 25 mins   Rest 10 mins

- 2 pork tenderloins (about 1 lb each)
- 2 tablespoons olive oil, divided
- ½ cup feta cheese, crumbled
- ¼ cup chopped fresh flat-leaf parsley
- 2 tablespoons chopped fresh rosemary
- 2 tablespoons chopped fresh thyme
- 3 cloves garlic, minced
- 2 tablespoons chopped sun-dried tomatoes
- 1 teaspoon sea salt
- ½ teaspoon black pepper
- ¼ teaspoon red pepper flakes (optional)
- 2 tablespoons balsamic vinegar
- 1 tablespoon honey
- Kitchen twine for tying
- Extra herbs for garnish

PREPARE THE PORK: Preheat the oven to 400 °F (204 °C). Butterfly each pork tenderloin by cutting lengthwise about ¾ of the way through along the center of the meat, then open like a book.

MAKE THE FILLING: Combine 1 tablespoon olive oil, feta cheese, parsley, rosemary, thyme, garlic, sun-dried tomatoes, salt, pepper, and red pepper flakes if using in a bowl. Mix well until combined.

STUFF AND ROLL: Spread the herb-cheese mixture evenly over the butterflied pork, leaving a 1-inch border, then roll tightly and secure with kitchen twine at 2-inch intervals.

SEAR THE PORK: Heat the remaining 1 tablespoon olive oil in a large oven-safe skillet over medium-high heat. Sear the stuffed tenderloins on all sides until golden brown, about 8-10 minutes total.

ROAST AND REST: Transfer the skillet to the oven and roast for 12-15 minutes until the internal temperature reaches 145 °F (63 °C). Remove from the oven, transfer the meat to a plate and let it rest uncovered for 10 minutes.

MAKE THE GLAZE: While the pork rests, place the same skillet over medium heat. Add the balsamic vinegar and honey to the pan juices, whisking until combined. Simmer for 2-3 minutes until slightly thickened. Brush the warm glaze generously over the rested pork tenderloin before slicing. Serve with any remaining glaze on the side.

Pair it with Côtes du Rhône red wine, Italian espresso with a touch of honey, or sparkling water with sliced grapes and fresh rosemary.

Butterflying creates a wider, flatter surface that's perfect for stuffing and ensures even cooking. Use a meat thermometer for accurate doneness. Tie securely with kitchen twine to prevent the filling from leaking during cooking.

FIRE & FEAST

TURKISH PIDE WITH SPICED CHICKEN

This traditional Turkish boat-shaped flatbread became my introduction to the art of making yeasted breads that are both practical and beautiful. The characteristic oval shape with pinched ends isn't just for looks—it creates perfect edges that hold the spiced topping and melted cheese while keeping the bottom crispy. The key is taking time to caramelize the onions properly and letting the dough develop. It's like making your own personal pizza, but with flavors that transport you straight to a Turkish market.

Serves 4 *Prep 25 mins* *Wait 1 hr* *Cook/Bake 40 mins*

For the Dough:

- 1 teaspoon active dry yeast
- 1 teaspoon sugar
- ¾ cup warm water
- 3 cups all-purpose flour
- 1 teaspoon sea salt
- 2 tablespoons olive oil
- 1 tablespoon plain yogurt

For the Chicken Filling:

- 1 lb boneless skinless chicken breast
- 2 tablespoons olive oil
- 1 large onion, chopped
- 3 cloves garlic, minced
- 1 teaspoon ground cumin
- 1 teaspoon paprika
- ½ teaspoon ground coriander
- ½ teaspoon red pepper flakes
- ½ teaspoon black pepper
- 1 teaspoon sea salt
- 1 small red bell pepper, chopped
- ¼ cup chopped flat-leaf parsley

For Assembly:

- ½ cup shredded mozzarella cheese
- 2 tablespoons unsalted butter
- 1 cup crumbled feta cheese
- Fresh parsley for garnish

MAKE THE DOUGH: Dissolve the yeast and sugar in warm water. Cover and set aside for 5 minutes until foamy. Mix in the flour, salt, olive oil, and yogurt to form a soft dough. Knead for 8 minutes until smooth. Place in an oiled bowl, cover with a damp towel, and let rise in a warm, dark place for 1 hour until doubled in size.

PREPARE THE FILLING: Chop the chicken breast into bite-sized pieces. Heat the olive oil in a large skillet over medium heat. Add the onions and ook them for 15 minutes until caramelized. Add garlic and sauté for 1-2 minutes until fragrant. Add the diced chicken, cumin, paprika, coriander, red pepper flakes, black pepper, and salt. Sauté for 10 minutes until the chicken is cooked through. Add the chopped red bell pepper and parsley.

ROLL THE DOUGH: Preheat the oven to 450 °F (232 °C). Divide the risen dough into 4 equal portions. Roll each into oval shapes about 8 inches long and 4 inches wide on a floured surface.

SHAPE AND BUILD THE PIDE: Place the 4 dough ovals on 2 parchment-lined sheet pans. Sprinkle the mozzarella cheese down the center of each oval, leaving a 1-inch border. Add the filling on top of the cheese. Pinch and twist the ends to create the traditional boat shape with raised edges.

BAKE: Melt the butter and brush the edges of the pides with it. Bake for 12-15 minutes until golden brown and the cheese is bubbling.

SERVE: Remove from the oven and garnish with feta cheese and parsley. Serve hot while the cheese is still melted and the bread is crispy.

Pair it with Turkish Öküzgözü red wine, Turkish raki with cold water and ice, or Turkish ayran (yogurt drink) with fresh mint.

Dough can be made a day ahead and refrigerated, brought to room temperature before shaping. Assemble the pides directly on the baking sheet, as they become difficult to transfer once filled. Don't overfill the pide or the edges won't seal properly.

BEEF STEW WITH PEARL ONIONS

A few years back, I was working with Michalis, a marketing person from Cyprus. During what was supposed to be a simple video call to discuss ideas, he apologized for needing to cook dinner for his family. I loved the informality of it all. I asked if he could position his phone so I could watch him cook while we talked. He was cooking a beef stew. Throughout our discussion, he casually described the ingredients he was adding—the way he browned the meat, layered in the vegetables, and built those deep flavors. Our call ended before the stew finished cooking, but it was the most fascinating experience. Later, I recreated this recipe from memory.

Serves 4   *Prep 25 mins*   *Cook 2 hrs*

- 2 tablespoons olive oil
- 2 lbs beef chuck roast, cut into 2-inch cubes
- 1 ½ teaspoons sea salt
- ½ teaspoon freshly ground black pepper
- 1 ½ tablespoons butter
- 1 lb pearl onions, peeled
- 1 lb small whole mushrooms (cremini or button)
- 3 large carrots, cut into 1-inch pieces
- 2 cloves garlic, minced
- 2 tablespoons all-purpose flour
- 3 cups beef broth
- 1 ½ cups red wine
- 2 bay leaves
- 2 sprigs fresh thyme
- 1 sprig fresh rosemary
- 1 cup fresh or frozen peas
- ¼ cup chopped fresh flat-leaf parsley

BROWN THE BEEF: Heat the olive oil in a large Dutch oven over medium-high heat. Season the beef cubes with salt and pepper and add them to the pot. Brown them on all sides for 8-10 minutes until deeply caramelized. Work in batches, if needed, to avoid overcrowding.

COOK THE VEGETABLES: Remove the beef and add butter to the same pot. Sauté the pearl onions, whole mushrooms, and carrots on medium-high heat for 5 minutes until lightly golden. Add minced garlic and sauté for 1 minute until fragrant.

BUILD THE STEW BASE: Sprinkle the flour over the vegetables and cook for 1 minute. Gradually add the beef broth and red wine, stirring to scrape up the browned bits from the bottom of the pot.

BRAISE THE STEW: Return the beef to the pot and add bay leaves, thyme, rosemary. Bring to a boil, then reduce heat to low, cover, and simmer for 1 hour 45 minutes until the beef is tender. Be sure to stir every 10 minutes.

FINISH AND SERVE: Add the peas during the last 10 minutes of cooking. Remove the bay leaves and herb sprigs. Taste and adjust the seasoning. Stir in the fresh parsley before serving hot in bowls.

Pair it with Côtes du Rhône, French press coffee with a touch of brandy, or sparkling water with rosemary and orange segments.

Don't skip browning the beef—it adds essential flavor depth to the entire stew. Add peas at the end to maintain their bright color and texture. Remove herb sprigs before serving for a clean presentation.

GROUND BEEF KEBABS WITH VEGETABLES

These flavorful ground beef kebabs became my solution when I wanted the taste of traditional Mediterranean kebabs but with the convenience of using ground meat instead of chunks. What I love about this recipe is how versatile it is—you can shape the seasoned ground meat into round meatballs or elongated sausage shapes, though I've found the meatball shape is much easier to handle on the grill pan. The colorful vegetables not only look beautiful but also cook perfectly alongside the meat, creating a complete meal on skewers.

Serves 4   Prep 25 mins   Grill 15 mins   Rest 5 mins

For the Beef Kebabs:
- 1½ lbs ground beef (80/20 blend)
- 1 medium onion, minced
- 3 cloves garlic, minced
- ¼ cup fresh flat-leaf parsley, chopped
- 2 teaspoons ground cumin
- 1 teaspoon smoked paprika
- 1 teaspoon dried oregano
- 1 teaspoon sea salt
- ½ teaspoon black pepper
- ¼ teaspoon cayenne pepper (optional)
- 2 tablespoons olive oil

For the Vegetables:
- 1 large red onion, cut into chunks
- 2 medium zucchini, sliced into thick rounds
- 2 cups cherry tomatoes
- 2 tablespoons olive oil
- ½ teaspoon sea salt
- ¼ teaspoon black pepper

For Serving:
- Fresh parsley for garnish
- Lemon wedges
- 8-10 wooden skewers

PREPARE THE SEASONED MEAT: In a large bowl, combine ground beef, minced onion, garlic, parsley, cumin, paprika, oregano, salt, pepper, and cayenne if using. Mix gently with your hands until just combined—don't overmix. Divide the mixture into 16-20 portions and shape into round meatballs.

PREPARE THE VEGETABLES: Toss the red onion chunks, zucchini rounds, and cherry tomatoes with olive oil, salt, and pepper.

ASSEMBLE THE SKEWERS: Thread the shaped meatballs alternately with vegetables onto soaked wooden skewers, leaving small spaces between pieces for even cooking.

COOK ON GRILL PAN: Heat a large grill pan over medium-high heat and brush with olive oil. Cook the kebabs for 12-15 minutes, turning every 3-4 minutes to ensure all sides are browned and the internal temperature reaches 160 °F (71 °C).

REST AND SERVE: Let the kebabs rest for 5 minutes, then garnish with fresh parsley and serve with lemon wedges for squeezing.

Pair with a bold red wine like Malbec, Turkish beer, or sparkling water with fresh mint and lemon.

Don't overmix the meat to keep the kebabs tender. Soak wooden skewers for at least 30 minutes to prevent burning.

MOROCCAN BRAISED CHICKEN WITH OLIVES

This aromatic chicken dish taught me how warming spices can completely transform a simple braised chicken into something that fills the kitchen with incredible aromas and tastes even better. The key is letting the spices bloom in the oil first—you can actually tell when they're ready by their fragrance, and that's when the magic happens. The combination of warm spices with briny olives and bright lemon creates this amazing balance of flavors that makes the whole house feel like something special is cooking. It's become one of my favorite cold-weather meals because it's both comforting and exotic at the same time.

Serves 4   Prep 15 mins   Cook 45 mins

- 3 tablespoons olive oil
- 6 chicken thighs, bone-in, skin-on
- 1 teaspoon sea salt
- ½ teaspoon black pepper
- 1 large onion, thinly sliced
- 1 tablespoon minced fresh ginger
- 4 cloves garlic, minced
- 1 teaspoon ground cinnamon
- 1 teaspoon ground ginger
- ½ teaspoon turmeric
- ½ teaspoon ground cumin
- ¼ teaspoon saffron threads
- 1 cup chicken broth
- 1 cup green olives, pitted
- 2 preserved lemons, quartered (or 2 lemons, sliced)
- ¼ cup chopped fresh cilantro
- ¼ cup chopped fresh flat-leaf parsley
- Lemon wedges for serving

BROWN THE CHICKEN: Heat the olive oil in a large Dutch oven over high heat. Season the chicken thighs with salt and pepper and brown skin-side down for 5 minutes until golden. Flip and brown for 3 minutes more. We'll finish cooking it later.

BUILD THE AROMATIC BASE: Remove the chicken and reduce heat to medium. Add the sliced onion to the same pot and cook for 5 minutes until softened. Add the minced ginger and garlic, cooking for 2 minute until fragrant.

BLOOM THE SPICES: Stir in the cinnamon, ground ginger, turmeric, cumin, and saffron, cooking for 30 seconds until aromatic. Add the chicken broth, scraping up the browned bits from the bottom.

BRAISE THE CHICKEN: Return the chicken to the pot skin-side up. Add the olives and preserved lemons and bring to a simmer. Cover and braise for 30 minutes until the chicken is tender and cooked through.

FINISH AND SERVE: Remove from heat, taste and adjust seasoning. Sprinkle with fresh cilantro and parsley before serving hot with lemon wedges and the aromatic braising liquid.

Pair it with Moroccan Côtes de Meknès red wine, traditional Moroccan mint tea with honey, or fresh orange juice with orange blossom water and sparkling water.

Don't skip browning the chicken for deep flavor development—it's essential for the rich base. Preserved lemons can be found in Middle Eastern stores or substituted with fresh lemon slices. Adjust spices to your taste preference.

PESTO CHICKEN WRAPPED IN LAVASH

This vibrant wrap turned into the perfect fusion of Italian and Middle Eastern traditions after I discovered how beautifully fresh basil pesto pairs with tender grilled chicken in soft lavash bread. I learned this combination from my Lebanese coworker, Zeina, who told me that the key is to warm the lavash just enough to make it pliable without losing its texture. The herbaceous intensity of homemade pesto coating the chicken creates an aromatic base that makes every bite sing with Mediterranean flavors.

For the Pesto:

- 2 cups fresh basil leaves, packed
- ¼ cup pine nuts, toasted
- 3 cloves garlic
- ½ cup extra virgin olive oil
- ½ cup Parmesan cheese, grated
- ¼ teaspoon sea salt
- ¼ teaspoon black pepper

For the Chicken:

- 1.5 lbs boneless, skinless chicken breasts
- 2 tablespoons olive oil
- 1 teaspoon sea salt
- ½ teaspoon black pepper
- ½ teaspoon dried oregano

For Assembly:

- 4 large lavash flatbreads
- 2 cups fresh arugula or spinach
- 1 large tomatoes, chopped
- 4 oz feta cheese, crumbled
- ¼ red onion, thinly sliced (optional)

Serves 4 Prep 25 mins Cook 15 mins Rest 5 mins

MAKE THE PESTO: Combine the basil leaves, toasted pine nuts, and garlic in a food processor. Pulse until roughly chopped. With the food processor running, slowly drizzle in the olive oil until smooth. Add the Parmesan cheese, salt, and pepper and pulse a few times to combine.

GRILL THE CHICKEN: Season the chicken breasts with olive oil, salt, pepper, and oregano. Grill on medium-high heat for 6-7 minutes per side until the internal temperature reaches 165 °F (74 °C). Let rest for 5 minutes before slicing into cubes.

COAT WITH PESTO: Toss the warm chicken cubes with ¾ of the prepared pesto until well-coated. Reserve the remaining pesto for spreading on the lavash bread.

PREPARE THE LAVASH BREAD: Warm the lavash bread briefly in a dry skillet or microwave for 15 seconds until pliable. Spread a thin layer of reserved pesto over the entire surface of each flatbread.

ASSEMBLE THE WRAPS: Layer each lavash with fresh arugula or spinach, pesto-coated chicken, chopped tomatoes, crumbled feta, and red onion slices if using down the center third of the flatbread.

ROLL AND SERVE: Fold the bottom edge up over the filling, then fold in the sides and roll tightly from bottom to create a secure wrap, cut in half diagonally for serving and secure with toothpicks if needed.

Pair it with Pinot Grigio or Vermentino white wine, Italian Aperol spritz with prosecco, or lemonade with sparkling water and mint.

Make pesto up to three days ahead and store it refrigerated with plastic wrap pressed directly on the surface. Chicken can be grilled a day before and stored refrigerated. Wrap the roll tightly in parchment paper for portable lunches or picnics.

SHEET PAN STEAK GYROS

This flavorful sheet pan version of traditional gyros became my answer to craving authentic Greek flavors without the special equipment. The key is using flank steak seasoned with classic Greek herbs and spices, then roasting it alongside colorful vegetables until everything caramelizes beautifully. What I love about this approach is how the steak stays tender while developing those crispy edges, and the vegetables get perfectly charred. You can serve it stuffed inside warm pita bread or with pita on the side for a more casual meal.

For the Steak:
- 3 tablespoons olive oil
- 3 cloves garlic, minced
- 2 teaspoons dried oregano
- 1 teaspoon ground cumin
- 1 teaspoon smoked paprika
- 1 teaspoon sea salt
- ½ teaspoon black pepper
- 1½ lbs flank steak

For the Tzatziki:
- 1 cucumber
- 1 cup Greek yogurt
- 2 cloves garlic, minced
- 2 tablespoons lemon juice
- 2 tablespoons chopped fresh mint
- 1 tablespoon olive oil
- ½ teaspoon sea salt

For the Vegetables:
- 1 large red onion, sliced
- 1 orange bell pepper, cut into strips
- 1 large zucchini, sliced into half-moons
- 2 tablespoons olive oil
- ½ teaspoon sea salt
- ¼ teaspoon black pepper
- 4-6 warm pita breads for serving

Serves 4   Prep 20 mins   Roast 25 mins   Rest 10 mins

MARINATE THE STEAK: Combine olive oil, minced garlic, oregano, cumin, paprika, salt, and pepper in a large bowl. Add the flank steak and rub the marinade all over. Let marinate at room temperature for 15 minutes.

MAKE THE TZATZIKI: Grate the cucumber and squeeze out excess water using a clean kitchen towel. Mix with Greek yogurt, minced garlic, lemon juice, mint, olive oil, and salt. Refrigerate until serving.

PREPARE FOR ROASTING: Preheat oven to 425 °F (218 °C). Line a medium baking sheet and another large baking sheet with parchment paper.

SEASON THE VEGETABLES: Toss the sliced onion, bell pepper, and zucchini with olive oil, salt, and pepper. Spread on the large prepared baking sheet.

ROAST EVERYTHING: Place the marinated steak on the medium prepared baking sheet. Place both baking sheets in the oven. Roast for 12-15 minutes for medium-rare, or until the internal temperature reaches 135 °F (57 °C). The vegetables should be tender and lightly charred.

REST, SLICE, AND SERVE: Remove from the oven and let the steak rest for 10 minutes. Slice thinly against the grain into strips. Arrange sliced steak and roasted vegetables on a platter with warm pita bread and tzatziki.

Pair with a crisp Greek white wine like Assyrtiko, a cold Greek beer, or sparkling water with lemon and fresh mint.

Slice the steak against the grain for maximum tenderness. For extra flavor, char the pita bread lightly on the grill or in a dry skillet before serving. Discard cucumber ends before grating, as they can be bitter.

FIRE & FEAST

GREEK CHICKEN SOUVLAKI

I discovered the magic of souvlaki lies in its beautiful simplicity—good chicken, a perfect marinade, and proper grilling technique. The marinade of olive oil, lemon, and oregano works together to tenderize the meat while infusing it with those bright, herbaceous flavors that define Greek cuisine. Paired with cooling lemon herb yogurt, these skewers deliver incredible flavor with surprisingly little effort.

For the Chicken:

- 2 lbs boneless, skinless chicken breasts
- ¼ cup olive oil
- 3 tablespoons lemon juice
- 2 tablespoons lemon zest
- 4 cloves garlic, minced
- 1 teaspoon dried oregano
- 1 teaspoon sea salt
- ½ teaspoon black pepper
- 2 tablespoons minced fresh flat-leaf parsley
- 8 wooden skewers

For the Lemon Herb Yogurt:

- ½ cup Greek yoghurt
- 2 tablespoons mayonnaise
- 1 teaspoon dijon mustard
- 1 tablespoon extra-virgin olive oil
- 2 tablespoons minced flat-leaf parsley
- 1 tablespoon minced mint
- 1 tablespoon lemon juice
- ½ teaspoon salt
- ¼ teaspoon black pepper

For Serving:

- Cherry tomatoes
- Fresh flat-leaf parsley
- Lemon wedges
- Warm pita bread

Serves 4   Prep 25 mins   Wait 2 hrs   Grill 12 mins

MARINATE THE CHICKEN: Cut the chicken breasts into 1-inch cubes. Combine the olive oil, lemon juice, lemon zest, minced garlic, oregano, salt, pepper, and parsley in a large bowl. Add the cubed chicken and toss to coat completely. Refrigerate for a minimum 2 hours for flavor development.

MAKE THE LEMON HERB YOGURT: In a medium bowl, whisk together the yogurt, mayonnaise, mustard, olive oil, parsley, mint, lemon juice, salt, and pepper. Refrigerate until ready to serve.

PREPARE FOR GRILLING: Soak the wooden skewers in water. Preheat the grill or grill pan to medium-high heat. Thread the marinated chicken onto the skewers, leaving small spaces between pieces for even cooking.

GRILL THE SKEWERS: Grill the skewers for 10-12 minutes total. Turn every 3 minutes to ensure all sides develop beautiful grill marks and the chicken reaches an internal temperature of 165 °F (74 °C).

REST AND SERVE: Remove from the grill and let rest for a few minutes. Arrange on a serving platter with cherry tomatoes. Garnish with fresh chopped parsley and serve with a bowl of lemon herb yogurt, lemon wedges, and warm pita bread for an authentic Greek presentation.

Pair it with Assyrtiko or Roditis white wine, Greek ouzo with ice and water, or lemonade with fresh mint and sparkling water.

Marinate at least 2 hours but no more than 8 hours to prevent texture changes. Soak wooden skewers in water for 30 minutes to prevent them from burning. Rub dried oregano between your palms before adding to release its oils and intensify the flavor.

BAKED CHEESE TORTELLINI WITH SAUSAGE

I developed this recipe for those times when I want to make something special that feeds a crowd without being too complicated. The combination of store-bought cheese-filled tortellini, Italian sausage, and melted cheese creates something hearty and satisfying that's perfect for weekend entertaining or Sunday family dinners. What I appreciate most is how everything bakes together in one dish—the pasta stays tender, the flavors meld beautifully, and the cheese on top gets golden and bubbly.

Serves 6   Prep 15 mins   Cook 26 mins   Bake 20 mins

- 2 tablespoons olive oil
- 1 lb Italian sausage (sweet or spicy), casings removed
- 1 medium onion, diced
- 4 cloves garlic, minced
- 2 tablespoons tomato paste
- 2 teaspoons dried oregano
- 1 teaspoon dried basil
- ½ teaspoon red pepper flakes
- 1 can (28 oz) crushed tomatoes
- 1 can (14 oz) diced tomatoes
- ½ cup red wine (optional)
- 1 teaspoon sea salt
- ½ teaspoon black pepper
- 2 tablespoons chopped fresh rosemary
- 1 package (20 oz) refrigerated cheese tortellini
- 8 oz fresh mozzarella, sliced
- ½ cup grated Parmesan cheese
- 2 tablespoons fresh basil

BROWN THE SAUSAGE: Heat the olive oil in a large oven-safe skillet over medium-high heat. Add the Italian sausage and cook, breaking it up with a spoon, for 6-8 minutes until browned and cooked through.

BUILD THE SAUCE: Add the diced onion to the same skillet and cook for 4-5 minutes until softened. Add the garlic and cook for 1 minute until fragrant.

ADD SEASONINGS AND TOMATOES: Stir in the tomato paste and sauté for 1 minute. Add the oregano, basil, and red pepper flakes and sauté for 30 seconds. Add crushed tomatoes, diced tomatoes, red wine if using, salt, and pepper. Bring to a simmer and cook for 10 minutes. Stir in the fresh rosemary.

ADD THE TORTELLINI: Add the uncooked tortellini to the same skillet, stirring gently to combine and coat the pasta.

ADD THE CHEESE: Preheat the oven to 375 °F (191 °C). Arrange the fresh mozzarella slices over the top of the tortellini. Sprinkle with grated Parmesan cheese.

BAKE UNTIL BUBBLY: Bake for 20 minutes until the cheese is melted and golden brown on top, the sauce is bubbling around the edges, and the tortellini is fully cooked. Garnish with fresh basil before serving hot.

Pair it with Sangiovese red wine, Italian chinotto with fresh herbs, or sparkling water with sliced grapes and basil.

To test if tortellini is done, remove a piece and taste—it should be tender without any doughy texture. If using frozen tortellini, rinse under hot running water in a colander and drain before using. Use an oven-safe skillet or transfer everything to a baking dish.

SHEET PAN GARLIC BUTTER CHICKEN & POTATOES

This rustic one-pan dish became my weeknight salvation when I discovered how roasting everything together creates extraordinary flavors with minimal effort. The secret is the herb butter—it melts and mingles with the chicken juices and potato starches to create this incredible sauce that coats everything. It's one of those meals that looks impressive but is incredibly simple, and cleanup is a breeze since everything cooks on one pan.

For the Chicken & Potatoes:

- 1 ½ lbs boneless, skinless chicken breasts
- ¼ cup olive oil
- 1 teaspoon sea salt
- ½ teaspoon black pepper
- 4 cloves garlic, minced
- 1 teaspoon dried oregano
- ¼ teaspoon paprika
- 1 ½ lbs baby potatoes, halved

For the Herb Butter:

- 4 tablespoons butter, melted
- 3 cloves garlic, minced
- ¼ cup chopped fresh basil
- 3 tablespoons chopped fresh flat-leaf parsley
- 2 tablespoons chopped fresh rosemary
- 1 tablespoon fresh thyme leaves
- ¼ teaspoon sea salt
- ¼ teaspoon red pepper flakes

For Finishing:

- 4 oz fresh mozzarella, torn into pieces
- Sprigs of fresh herbs
- Lemon wedges for serving

Serves 4   Prep 20 mins   Wait 15 mins   Roast 30 mins

MARINATE THE CHICKEN: Cut the chicken breast into 2-inch cubes. Add the chicken to a large bowl with olive oil, salt, pepper, minced garlic, oregano, and paprika. Toss to coat the chicken pieces. Set aside for 15 minutes to marinate.

PREPARE THE HERB BUTTER: Combine the melted butter with minced garlic, basil, parsley, rosemary, thyme, salt, and red pepper flakes in a small bowl. Mix well and set aside.

PREPARE FOR ROASTING: While chicken is marinating, preheat the oven to 425 °F (218 °C). Add the halved potatoes to the chicken and toss until coated. Spread the chicken and potatoes on a large rimmed sheet pan in a single layer for proper browning.

START ROASTING: Roast for 20 minutes. Remove the sheet pan from the oven. Reduce the oven temperature to 350 °F (177 °C). Brush the chicken and potatoes generously with the prepared herb butter. Return to the oven and continue roasting for 10 minutes until the chicken reaches 165 °F (74 °C) internal temperature.

ADD CHEESE AND SERVE: Remove from the oven and immediately scatter the torn mozzarella pieces over the hot chicken and potatoes, allowing the residual heat to slightly melt the cheese. Garnish with herbs and serve with lemon wedges directly from the sheet pan.

Pair it with Montepulciano d'Abruzzo red wine, Italian limoncello with sparkling water, or rosemary lemonade with ice.

Cut potatoes uniformly for even cooking. Fresh herbs in the butter make a significant difference in flavor compared to dried ones. Don't overcrowd the pan—use two sheet pans if necessary for proper browning. Line the sheet pan with foil for easy cleanup.

HONEY & HERITAGE
Desserts that Capture the Sunshine

CHOCOLATE ORANGE MOUSSE

This luxurious mousse came about when I wanted to try something different with chocolate dessert. The combination of dark chocolate with fresh orange zest creates this amazing contrast—the silky, velvety texture melts on your tongue while the vibrant citrus cuts through the richness perfectly. The mousse sets beautifully in individual glasses, making each serving feel like a special treat. I love making this for dinner parties because it can be prepared ahead of time.

For the Mousse:

- 6 oz dark chocolate (70% cocoa), chopped
- 3 tablespoons unsalted butter
- 3 large eggs, yolk & white separated
- 2 tablespoons fresh orange juice
- 1 tablespoon orange zest
- 1 teaspoon vanilla extract
- ⅛ teaspoon sea salt
- ¼ cup granulated sugar, divided
- 1 cup heavy cream

For Garnish:

- Candied orange peels or fresh orange segments

Serves 6   Prep 30 mins   Cook 0 mins   Chill 4 hrs

MAKE THE CHOCOLATE BASE: Combine the chopped dark chocolate and butter in a microwave-safe bowl. Heat in 15-second intervals. Stir between each interval until the chocolate is smooth and glossy, taking care not to burn the chocolate. Cool slightly and whisk in the egg yolks one at a time until well combined.

ADD THE ORANGE FLAVORS: Stir in the orange juice, orange zest, vanilla extract, and salt into the chocolate base and mix to combine.

WHIP THE EGG WHITES: Beat the egg whites in a clean bowl until soft peaks form. Gradually add half the sugar and continue beating until stiff, glossy peaks form, being careful not to overbeat.

WHIP THE CREAM: In a separate bowl, whip the heavy cream with the remaining sugar until soft peaks form.

FOLD TOGETHER: Gently fold one-third of the beaten egg whites into the chocolate mixture to lighten it. Then fold in the whipped cream, followed by the remaining egg whites, working carefully to maintain the airiness.

CHILL AND SERVE: Divide the mousse among six serving glasses or bowls. Cover with plastic wrap and refrigerate for at least 4 hours until set. Garnish with candied orange peels or fresh segments just before serving.

Pair it with Port or orange Muscat wine, Grand Marnier or Italian Aperol, or strong espresso with a twist of orange peel.

Use room temperature eggs for easier incorporation and better volume when whipping egg whites. Fresh orange juice provide much brighter flavor than bottled alternatives. Mousse can be made up to two days ahead but add garnishes just before serving.

HONEY PANNA COTTA

I first discovered this silky dessert at a small Mediterranean restaurant in Palo Alto, California on my birthday a few years back. When they brought it to the table with a candle, the panna cotta was so delicate and wobbly that it could barely hold the candle upright—I was amazed by how something so ethereal could taste so rich and satisfying. That inspired me to recreate it at home, transforming honey's natural sweetness into this cloud-like custard that captures everything I love about Mediterranean desserts.

For the Panna Cotta:
- 1 packet (2 ¼ teaspoons) unflavored gelatin
- 3 tablespoons warm water
- 2 cups heavy cream
- ½ cup whole milk
- ⅓ cup honey
- 1 teaspoon vanilla extract

For the Honey Sauce:
- ¼ cup honey
- 2 tablespoons warm water
- 1 tablespoon lemon juice
- ¼ teaspoon vanilla extract
- ⅛ teaspoon sea salt

For Garnish:
- ¼ cup sliced almonds, toasted (optional)

Serves 6 Prep 20 mins Cook 5 mins Chill 4 hrs

BLOOM THE GELATIN: Sprinkle the gelatin over warm water in a small bowl and let bloom for 5 minutes until softened. Microwave for 15 seconds or until completely dissolved and clear.

HEAT THE DAIRY BASE: Heat the cream, milk, and honey in a medium saucepan over medium heat. Stir frequently until the honey dissolves and the mixture is hot but not boiling, about 5 minutes.

COMBINE AND STRAIN: Remove from heat and whisk in the dissolved gelatin and vanilla extract until completely smooth. Strain the mixture through a fine-mesh sieve to remove any lumps.

SET THE PANNA COTTA: Divide the mixture evenly among six 4-ounce ramekins or molds. Cover the ramekins with plastic wrap and refrigerate for at least 4 hours or overnight until completely set and firm.

MAKE THE HONEY SAUCE: Whisk together the honey, warm water, lemon juice, vanilla extract, and salt until smooth. Adjust the consistency with additional water if needed for a pourable texture.

DRIZZLE AND SERVE: To serve, dip the bottom of each ramekin briefly in warm water and run a knife around the edges. Invert onto serving plates and drizzle with honey sauce. Garnish with toasted almonds if using.

Pair it with Moscato d'Asti or Greek Samos dessert wine, Italian grappa with honey, or chamomile tea with fresh mint and honey.

Use high-quality honey with distinct floral notes for best flavor development. Bloom gelatin properly to ensure smooth texture without grittiness. Panna cotta can be made up to two days ahead and kept covered in the refrigerator.

LEMON SUGAR COOKIES WITH OLIVE OIL

These tender, citrus-scented cookies combine bright lemon and fruity olive oil in a way that's totally different from traditional butter cookies. A few years back, I first made them for Firefighters Appreciation Day on May 4th and took them down to our local fire station. The firefighters loved them so much that now I don't wait for May 4th—whenever I feel like baking, I make a big batch and drop them off. One of the firefighters who bakes told me he thinks the olive oil creates a more delicate crumb than butter, and I was so impressed that he noticed this.

Makes 24 cookies   Prep 20 mins   Bake 12 mins

For the Cookies:
- 2 ½ cups all-purpose flour
- ½ teaspoon baking powder
- ½ teaspoon baking soda
- ½ teaspoon sea salt
- 1 cup granulated sugar
- ½ cup extra virgin olive oil
- 2 large eggs
- 2 tablespoons fresh lemon juice
- 1 tablespoon lemon zest
- 1 teaspoon vanilla extract

For Rolling:
- 2 tablespoons granulated sugar
- 1 teaspoon lemon zest
- 4 tablespoons powdered sugar

PREPARE FOR BAKING: Preheat the oven to 350 °F (177 °C). Line two large sheet pans with parchment paper. Whisk together the flour, baking powder, baking soda, and salt in a medium bowl. Set it aside.

MAKE THE DOUGH: Beat the granulated sugar with olive oil in a large bowl using an electric mixer until well combined. Add the eggs one at a time. Add lemon juice, lemon zest, and vanilla extract, mixing until smooth.

COMBINE INGREDIENTS: Gradually add the dry ingredients to the wet ingredients, mixing just until combined to form a soft. It'll be a slightly sticky dough that holds together when pressed.

SHAPE AND COAT: On a small plate, mix granulated sugar with lemon zest. Scoop the dough into 1 1/2-inch balls using a cookie scoop or spoon. Roll each ball first in powdered sugar, then in the lemon zest-sugar mixture for a double coating that creates a beautiful crackled appearance.

BAKE THE COOKIES: Place the coated dough balls on the prepared sheet pans spacing 2 inches apart. Bake for 10-12 minutes until the edges are set and the tops have developed characteristic cracks but the centers still look slightly underbaked.

COOL AND SERVE: Cool on the sheet pans for 5 minutes before transferring to wire racks, allowing the cookies to finish setting while maintaining their tender, soft texture throughout.

Pair it with Limoncello or Italian Moscato d'Asti, espresso with a touch of lemon zest, or sparkling water with lemon and thyme.

Use high-quality extra virgin olive oil with mild, fruity flavor rather than robust or peppery varieties. Fresh lemon zest provides much brighter flavor than dried alternatives. Cookies are best eaten within three days when stored in airtight containers.

ORANGE & ALMOND CAKE

A few years ago, I decided I was done bringing home those overly sweet, artificially colored birthday cakes for my husband's birthday. Instead, I baked this orange and almond cake, and it was such a hit that we've never bought another store-bought birthday cake since. This version uses whole cooked oranges that get pureed into the batter, creating an incredibly moist cake with intense orange flavor throughout. It's become our celebration cake for every special occasion, and I love how it tastes even better the next day.

For the Oranges:
- 2 medium oranges, whole and unpeeled
- Water for boiling

For the Cake:
- 6 large eggs
- 1 cup granulated sugar
- 2½ cups almond flour
- 1 teaspoon baking powder
- ½ teaspoon sea salt

For Topping:
- Powdered sugar for dusting
- ¼ cup sliced toasted almonds

Serves 10   Prep 20 mins   Cook 45 mins   Bake 45 mins

PREPARE THE ORANGES: Place whole oranges in a large pot and cover with water. Bring to a boil and cook for 45 minutes until very tender. Drain and let cool. Cut the oranges into quarters, remove seeds, then puree the entire oranges (including peel) in a food processor until smooth.

PREPARE THE PAN: Preheat the oven to 350 °F (177 °C). Grease a 9-inch springform tin and line the bottom with parchment paper.

MAKE THE BATTER: In a large bowl, beat eggs and sugar with an electric mixer for 5 minutes until thick and pale. Fold in the orange puree until well combined.

ADD DRY INGREDIENTS: In a separate bowl, whisk together almond flour, baking powder, and salt. Gently fold the dry ingredients into the orange mixture until just combined.

BAKE THE CAKE: Pour batter into the prepared tin and smooth the top. Bake for 45 minutes until golden brown and a toothpick inserted in the center comes out clean.

COOL AND FINISH: Cool in the pan for 15 minutes before removing the sides of the springform tin. Cool completely on a wire rack. Dust with powdered sugar and sprinkle sliced toasted almonds before serving.

Pair it with Moscato d'Asti or Spanish late-harvest wine, Italian amaretto liqueur, or sparkling water with orange juice & rosemary.

The oranges can be cooked a day ahead and stored refrigerated. Make sure to puree the entire orange including the peel for maximum flavor. The cake is naturally gluten-free thanks to the almond flour base.

HONEY YOGURT WITH WALNUTS & FIGS

This simple dessert became my favorite way to use fresh figs from the farmer's market when they're perfectly ripe and sweet. My mom used to love figs, and whenever I make this dessert I somehow feel closer to her. There's something so satisfying about the combination of cool yogurt with warm honey, crunchy walnuts, and those soft, jammy figs. It's become my go-to dessert when I want something that feels special but naturally wholesome.

Serves 4   Prep 15 mins   Cook 4 mins

For the Yogurt:
- 2 cups Greek yogurt, full-fat
- ¼ cup honey (preferably Greek or wildflower)
- ½ teaspoon vanilla extract
- ⅛ teaspoon sea salt

For the Toppings:
- ½ cup walnuts, roughly chopped
- 8 fresh figs, sliced into rounds
- 3 tablespoons honey for drizzling
- 2 teaspoons extra virgin olive oil (optional)
- Fresh mint leaves for garnish
- 1 tablespoon orange zest (optional)

PREPARE THE YOGURT: Whisk together the Greek yogurt, honey, vanilla extract, and salt in a medium bowl until smooth and well combined, adjusting sweetness to taste.

TOAST THE WALNUTS: Toast the walnuts in a dry skillet over medium heat for 3-4 minutes until fragrant and lightly golden, stirring frequently to prevent burning. Set aside to cool completely.

ASSEMBLE THE BASE: Divide the yogurt mixture evenly among four serving bowls, creating smooth, even layers that will serve as the creamy foundation for the toppings.

ADD THE TOPPINGS: Arrange the fresh fig slices decoratively over the yogurt in each bowl, overlapping slightly for visual appeal, then sprinkle the toasted walnuts generously over the figs.

FINISH AND SERVE: Complete each serving with a generous drizzle of honey, a light drizzle of extra virgin olive oil if using for richness, fresh mint leaves, and orange zest if using. Serve immediately while the figs are at peak freshness.

Pair it with Moschofilero or Vinsanto dessert wine, Greek Metaxa brandy, or chamomile tea with honey and fresh mint.

Choose figs that are ripe but still firm for best texture and easy slicing without mushiness. Greek yogurt provides ideal thick consistency for this dessert. Toast walnuts just before serving to maintain maximum crunchiness.

PISTACHIO GELATO

I fell in love with pistachio gelato while visiting Florence, Italy, and knew I had to try recreating that incredible flavor at home. The gelato I had there was so rich and nutty, with this amazing creamy texture that was completely different from regular ice cream. It took me a couple of tries to get it right—the first batch was too icy, and the second was too sweet—but when I finally nailed it, I was transported right back to those narrow cobblestone streets. The key is to be patient with the churning process to get the dense, creamy texture.

For the Gelato Base:

- 1 ½ cups shelled unsalted raw pistachios
- 2 cups whole milk, divided
- 1 cup heavy cream
- ¾ cup granulated sugar, divided
- 6 large egg yolks
- ⅛ teaspoon sea salt
- 1 teaspoon vanilla extract
- 2 drops natural green food coloring (optional)

For Garnish:

- ½ cup shelled unsalted pistachios

Serves 8   Prep 40 mins   Cook 15 mins   Chill 6 hrs

PREPARE THE PISTACHIOS: Soak the pistachios in hot water for 10 minutes. Drain and rub with a clean kitchen towel to remove the skins. Blend the pistachios with 1/2 cup milk to form a smooth paste, about 3 minutes.

HEAT THE DAIRY BASE: Heat the remaining 1 1/2 cups milk, cream, and half the sugar in a heavy saucepan over medium heat until steaming and the sugar dissolves. Slowly whisk the hot mixture into the pistachio paste until completely smooth.

MAKE THE CUSTARD: Whisk the egg yolks with the remaining sugar and salt in a large bowl until pale and thick. Gradually add the hot pistachio mixture while whisking constantly to prevent curdling.

COOK THE CUSTARD: Return the mixture to the saucepan and cook over low heat. Stir constantly with a wooden spoon until the custard coats the back of the spoon and reaches 170 °F (77 °C), about 8 minutes.

CHILL THE BASE: Strain the custard through a fine-mesh sieve. Stir in the vanilla and food color if using. Cover with plastic wrap pressed directly on the surface and refrigerate for at least 2 hours until totally chilled.

FREEZE THE GELATO: Pour the chilled mixture into a shallow metal pan and freeze for 45 minutes. Remove from the freezer and vigorously whisk with a fork to break up ice crystals. Repeat this process every 30-45 minutes for 4 hours until the mixture is smooth and scoopable. Garnish with pistachios and serve.

Pair it with Sicilian Moscato or Passito dessert wine, Italian amaretto liqueur, or strong espresso with a touch of pistachio syrup.

Use good quality pistachios like Sicilian for an authentic flavor and vibrant natural color. Removing pistachio skins is crucial for smooth texture and prevents bitter aftertaste. If using an ice cream maker, churn according to the manufacturer's instructions.

CRUNCHY ALMOND BUTTER STUFFED DATES

When our son was growing up, we always had all kinds of nut butters in our home, and my favorite was the crunchy almond butter—I used to put it on everything. That's how this idea came to be when I had some beautiful Medjool dates and wondered what would happen if I filled them with almond butter. One bite and I was hooked—the natural sweetness of the dates combined with creamy almond butter creates this perfect little treat. Adding a drizzle of dark chocolate and a pinch of flaky sea salt makes them feel fancy enough to serve to friends.

For the Stuffed Dates:

- 12 large Medjool dates, pitted
- ½ cup crunchy natural almond butter, at room temperature
- 1 tablespoon honey (optional)

For the Drizzle:

- 4 oz dark chocolate (50% cocoa), chopped
- 1 tablespoon coconut oil

For the Topping:

- ¼ cup dried goji berries, chopped
- 1 teaspoon flaky sea salt
- Fresh mint leaves for garnish

Serves 6   *Prep 20 mins*   *Cook 5 mins*

PREPARE THE DATES: Carefully slice each date lengthwise with a sharp knife and gently open the date to create a pocket for stuffing without tearing the fruit.

STUFF THE DATES: In a small bowl, mix almond butter and honey if using. Fill each date cavity with about 2 teaspoons of almond butter filling, using a small spoon or piping bag to create an even fill. Gently press the date closed around the filling while leaving some filling visible.

MELT THE CHOCOLATE: Combine the chopped dark chocolate and coconut oil in a microwave-safe bowl. Heat in 15-second intervals. Stir between each interval until the chocolate is smooth and glossy, taking care not to burn the chocolate.

ARRANGE AND DRIZZLE: Place the stuffed dates on a parchment paper-lined serving platter. Use a spoon to drizzle the melted chocolate over each date in artistic patterns, allowing some chocolate to pool around the dates on the parchment.

FINISH AND SERVE: Immediately sprinkle the chopped goji berries and flaky sea salt over the chocolate while still wet. Add small mint leaves as garnish. Refrigerate for 10 minutes to set the chocolate before serving.

Pair it with Turkish coffee, Greek dessert wine like Samos Muscat, or sparkling water with orange blossom and fresh mint.

Check for pits inside the dates even if the package says they are pitted. Stuffed dates can be prepared up to two days ahead and stored covered in the refrigerator. Chocolate drizzling should be done just before serving for best appearance.

RICE PUDDING WITH ROSE PETALS

This recipe came about when I wanted to explore Middle Eastern flavors in my own kitchen. When I first tried rice pudding with rose water and pistachios, I was amazed by how elegant it tasted. The rose water gives it this delicate floral note that's unlike any other dessert, and the pistachios add this lovely crunch and color. It's perfect for when I want to serve something that feels exotic but is actually quite simple to make.

Serves 4 Prep 15 mins Cook 35 mins Chill 2 hrs

For the Rice Pudding:
- ¾ cup short-grain rice (such as Arborio)
- 3 cups whole milk
- ¾ cup heavy cream
- ½ cup granulated sugar
- ⅛ teaspoon sea salt
- 1 small cinnamon stick
- ½ teaspoon vanilla extract
- 4 teaspoons rose water
- ¼ teaspoon ground cardamom

For Garnish:
- ¼ cup shelled unsalted roasted pistachios
- 2 tablespoons dried edible rose petals

START THE PUDDING: Rinse the rice under cold water until the water runs clear. Combine with milk, cream, sugar, salt, and cinnamon stick in a large heavy-bottomed saucepan. Bring to a gentle boil over medium heat while stirring frequently.

SIMMER UNTIL CREAMY: Reduce heat to low and simmer uncovered for 30 minutes, stirring regularly to prevent sticking. Cook until the rice is tender and the pudding has thickened to a creamy consistency that coats the back of a spoon.

ADD AROMATICS: Remove from heat and discard the cinnamon stick. Stir in the vanilla extract, rose water, and ground cardamom.

CHILL THE PUDDING: Divide the warm pudding among four serving glasses or bowls. Cover the surface with plastic wrap pressed directly against the pudding to prevent skin forming. Refrigerate for at least 2 hours until completely chilled.

GARNISH AND SERVE: Chop the pistachios roughly. Just before serving, remove the plastic wrap and top each pudding with a generous sprinkle of pistachios and rose petals. Serve immediately while the garnishes maintain their vibrant colors and textures.

Pair it with Turkish Muscat dessert wine, Persian rosewater tea, or pomegranate juice with sparkling water and fresh mint.

Purchase dried edible rose petals from specialty spice shops or Middle Eastern markets ensuring they're food-grade. Rose water intensity varies by brand, so start with less and add gradually. Pudding can be made two days ahead but add garnishes just before serving.

BAKLAVA WITH PISTACHIOS & HONEY

My first baklava attempt was a complete disaster. The phyllo dough kept tearing, the butter wasn't spread evenly, and it looked nothing like those beautiful golden layers I was hoping for. I was so frustrated I almost gave up. After some practice, my third attempt turned out much better. Don't worry if yours doesn't look perfect the first time—even wonky baklava tastes incredible, and each attempt teaches you something new about working with that delicate phyllo dough.

Makes 24 pieces   Prep 1 hr   Bake 45 mins   Wait 4 hrs

For the Filling:

- 3 cups unsalted raw pistachios, chopped
- ¼ cup granulated sugar
- ½ teaspoon ground cinnamon
- ¼ teaspoon ground cloves
- ⅛ teaspoon sea salt

For Assembly:

- 1 package (1 lb) phyllo pastry, thawed
- 1 cup unsalted butter, melted
- ½ cup pistachios, chopped for topping

For the Syrup:

- 1 cup honey
- ½ cup granulated sugar
- ½ cup water
- 1 small cinnamon stick
- 2 whole cloves
- 2 tablespoons fresh lemon juice
- 1 teaspoon vanilla extract

PREPARE THE FILLING: Preheat the oven to 350 °F (177 °C). Prepare the nut filling by combining the chopped pistachios, sugar, cinnamon, cloves, and salt in a bowl, mixing until evenly distributed.

LAYER THE BOTTOM: Brush a 9x13 inch baking dish with melted butter. Place one phyllo sheet in the dish and brush it with melted butter. Add the second sheet on top and brush with butter again. Continue this process until you have layered 8 phyllo sheets, each brushed with butter.

ADD FILLING LAYERS: Sprinkle half of the nut mixture evenly over the phyllo base. Layer 8 more phyllo sheets on top, brushing each sheet with butter as you go. Spread the remaining nut mixture over it. Finish the top layers with all remaining phyllo sheets. Make sure to brush each individual sheet with butter before adding the next one.

SCORE AND BAKE: Brush the top layer generously with butter. Score into diamond or square shapes using a sharp knife, cutting through all layers. Bake for 40-45 minutes until golden brown and crispy.

PREPARE SYRUP: Combine honey, sugar, water, cinnamon stick, cloves, and lemon juice in a saucepan. Simmer for 10 minutes on medium-low heat. Add vanilla extract and stir.

FINISH AND REST: Pour the hot syrup evenly over the hot baklava, allowing it to soak completely. Sprinkle with chopped pistachios and cool for at least 4 hours before cutting and serving.

Pair it with Greek Muscat or Samos dessert wine, strong Turkish coffee, or traditional mint tea with honey.

While working, keep phyllo covered with a damp towel to prevent drying and cracking.

Since honey is the dominant flavor, use high-quality honey. Baklava improves with time.

Can be stored at room temperature for up to 5 days or refrigerated for up to 2 weeks.

CUSTARD PIE WITH FIGS & HONEY

My mom loved figs, so any dish that includes them holds a special place in my heart. This custard pie combines the silky, comforting texture of vanilla custard with beautiful fresh figs and golden honey. The smooth, creamy filling contrasts perfectly with the sweet, jammy fig slices on top. The honey brings out the natural fruit flavors beautifully, creating something that feels both elegant and comforting—ideal for when you want dessert to feel really special.

For the Pie Crust:
- 1 ¼ cups all-purpose flour
- ¼ teaspoon sea salt
- ½ cup cold unsalted butter, cubed
- 3-4 tablespoons ice water

For the Custard:
- 1 ½ cups heavy cream
- ½ cup whole milk
- 4 large eggs
- ⅓ cup granulated sugar
- ¼ cup honey
- 1 teaspoon vanilla extract
- ⅛ teaspoon sea salt
- ⅛ teaspoon nutmeg

For Topping:
- 5 fresh figs, sliced into 1/4-inch rounds
- 2 tablespoons honey for drizzling

Serves 8   Prep 30 mins   Wait 2 hr 30 mins   Bake 50 mins

MAKE THE PIE CRUST: Combine the flour and salt in a large bowl. Cut in the cold butter using a pastry cutter or two knives, working it into the flour until the mixture resembles coarse crumbs with some pea-sized pieces. Gradually add ice water, one tablespoon at a time, until the dough comes together. Wrap in plastic and chill for 30 minutes.

PREPARE THE PIE CRUST: Preheat the oven to 375 °F (191 °C). Roll the chilled dough into a 12-inch circle. Place it into a 9-inch pie pan and crimp the edges decoratively. Prick the bottom with a fork to prevent puffing.

BLIND BAKE: Line the pie crust with parchment paper and fill with dried beans to weigh it down. Blind bake for 15 minutes. Remove the beans and parchment paper and bake for 5 minutes until lightly golden. Remove the crust from the oven. Reduce the oven temperature to 325 °F (163 °C).

PREPARE THE CUSTARD: While the crust is baking, whisk together the cream, milk, eggs, sugar, honey, vanilla, salt, and nutmeg in a large bowl until smooth and well combined.

BAKE THE PIE: Pour the custard into the pre-baked crust and bake for 30 minutes. Remove and cool completely on a wire rack for at least 2 hours.

FINISH AND SERVE: Just before serving, slice the fresh figs into rounds and arrange decoratively over the cooled custard. Drizzle the entire pie with honey for a glossy, elegant finish.

Pair it with late-harvest Riesling or Sauternes, French Muscat dessert wine, or chamomile tea with honey and fresh mint.

You can use store-bought frozen pie crust instead of homemade and follow the same blind baking instructions. Remove the pie when the center still has a slight jiggle, as the custard continues cooking from residual heat.

Acknowledgments

To Subrao Shenoy, my beloved husband and the most adventurous taste-tester a cookbook author could ask for—your unwavering support and willingness to try hundreds of kitchen experiments have been the cornerstone of bringing these recipes to life. Thank you for loving me unconditionally and for standing beside me through every triumph and challenge of my culinary journey, from perfectly seasoned successes to the occasional burnt offering.

To my parents, Dr. Anant and Sudha Bhadri, who taught me the deepest truths about dedication through their daily lives. Within the walls of our modest childhood home in rural India, they created an extraordinary testament to devotion—my father, a brilliant physician, who built the area's only hospital, whose kindness reached countless underprivileged souls, and my mother, whose gift for transforming simple ingredients into expressions of love showed me that wonder exists in life's most fundamental acts of care. This book honors their enduring legacy and the countless meals shared around our little family table.

To my sister, Meena Timblo, who shares my passion for the culinary arts and understands that food is culture, memory, and love made tangible. Our conversations about food, flavors, and the stories bring such joy to my culinary journey. Thank you for being the one person who truly understands my obsession with cooking.

To Mary De Guzman, the talented artist responsible for the captivating cover that perfectly conveys the heart of this culinary journey. I remain deeply appreciative of your artistry, your meticulous formatting of the book, and for giving tangible form to what once existed only in my kitchen and imagination.

To the Mediterranean—land of timeless beauty, passionate cooks, and sun-drenched inspiration. Your ancient olive groves, bustling markets, and time-honored food traditions have inspired me to share these authentic flavors. Your spirit of generosity flows through these pages like olive oil over fresh bread—warming, nourishing, and inviting readers to gather around the table.

Seema

About The Author

Seema Shenoy is a passionate home chef who believes in the transformative power of food to bring people together. For over forty years, she has called the San Francisco Bay Area home with her husband - her pillar of strength. Their enduring partnership has taught her that true love is often expressed through nourishing those we cherish.

The Mediterranean has captured Seema's heart in a way she never anticipated. With her Indian heritage, she discovered a beautiful kinship between Mediterranean and Indian cuisines - both celebrate layering spices, slow cooking, and the deep connection between food and family. This shared philosophy compelled her to create this cookbook that honors authentic Mediterranean flavors.

A devoted mother, Seema finds immense joy in her relationship with her son and daughter-in-law. Her passion for nurturing extends naturally to cooking, where she believes every meal is an expression of love made tangible. You'll often find her experimenting with flavors and turning ordinary moments into cherished memories.

Seema develops her recipes at local farmers markets, discovering fresh seasonal ingredients. Surrounded by ripe tomatoes, fragrant herbs, and cheerful vendors, she finds inspiration for dishes that celebrate both simplicity and flavor.

In her cooking, as in her life, Seema celebrates the extraordinary beauty found in ordinary moments of connection. She believes that the greatest meals are created through the simple acts of love that sustain families and friendships through shared food and traditions.

Index

A
Aioli, garlic, 49
Artichoke hearts, braised with herbs, 102
Artichoke soup, lemon & spinach, 86
Artichoke spinach mini frittata, 26
Arugula salad with pears & blue cheese, 115
Avocado toast, fried eggs, 11

B
Baklava with pistachios & honey, 178
Balsamic glaze, 40
Bean purée, white, 52
Beef stew with pearl onions, 144
Breakfast pockets, egg & cheese, 27
Breakfast wraps, egg whites & feta, 15
Bruschetta, heirloom tomato caprese, 40

C
Caprese panini, 87
Carrot lentil soup, Moroccan, 95
Cauliflower, roasted with chermoula, 114
Cauliflower shawarma bowl, 90
Chickpea fries, crispy, 33
Chickpea flour pancakes, savory, 41
Chicken:
   braised Moroccan with olives, 148
   grain & chicken bowl, Mediterranean, 137
   Greek lemon rice soup with, 133
   grilled lemon pesto, 129
   pesto wrapped in lavash, 149
   sheet pan garlic butter with potatoes, 157
   souvlaki, Greek, 153
   spiced, stuffed eggplant with, 128
   Turkish pide with spiced, 141
Chocolate orange mousse, 162
Cod fritters, red onion & parsley, 66
Cookies, lemon sugar with olive oil, 166
Crostini, fig & goat cheese, 36
Crunchy almond butter stuffed dates, 174
Custard pie with figs & honey, 179

D
Dates, crunchy almond butter stuffed, 174
Deviled eggs, smoked salmon, 57
Dill sauce, 74
Dip, roasted red pepper, 45

E
Egg & cheese breakfast pockets, 27
Egg whites & feta breakfast wraps, 15
Eggplant:
   baked pasta with & tomatoes, 107
   grilled rolls, 99
   Parmesan on garlic bread, 122
   stuffed with spiced chicken, 128

F
Fennel & orange salad, 98
Feta, pan-fried with spiced herb honey, 44
Fig & goat cheese crostini, 36
Fish fillets, herb & Parmesan crusted, 78
Frittata, artichoke spinach mini, 26
Fritters:
   cod with red onion & parsley, 66
   zucchini with herb yogurt, 53

G
Gazpacho, roasted heirloom tomato, 110
Gelato, pistachio, 171
Granola, honey, 22
Greek dishes:
   chicken souvlaki, 153
   lemon rice soup with chicken, 133
   potato gratin with Kalamata olives, 103
   savory pancakes with scallions, 14
   yogurt parfait with honey granola, 22
Green beans, Lebanese in tomato sauce, 111
Green shakshuka with spinach, 19
Grilled salmon with Greek salad, 63
Ground beef kebabs with vegetables, 145

H
Halibut, pan-seared with lemon & capers, 67
Herb & Parmesan crusted fish fillets, 78
Herb-crusted lamb chops, 136
Herb sauce, 74
Herb yogurt, 53
Honey granola, 22
Honey panna cotta, 163
Honey yogurt with walnuts & figs, 170

K
Kebabs, ground beef with vegetables, 145

L
Lamb chops, herb-crusted, 136
Lebanese green beans in tomato sauce, 111
Lemon & caper sauce, 67
Lemon sugar cookies with olive oil, 166
Light pasta with lemon & garlic, 91

M
Meatballs:
   mini with herbed yogurt sauce, 32
   turkey in herb cream sauce, 132
Mediterranean grain & chicken bowl, 137
Menemen - Turkish scrambled eggs, 18
Moroccan dishes:
   braised chicken with olives, 148
   carrot lentil soup, 95
Mousse, chocolate orange, 162
Mushroom & herbed goat cheese tarts, 37
Mushrooms, stuffed portobello, 106
Mussels in white wine & garlic, 71

O
Olives, crispy fried with garlic aioli, 49
Omelet:
   Mediterranean with spinach & olives, 23
   Spanish with potatoes, 10
Orange & almond cake, 167

P
Paella, Spanish seafood, 79
Pancakes:
   Greek savory with scallions, 14
   savory chickpea flour, 41
Pan-fried feta with spiced herb honey, 44
Pan-seared halibut with lemon & capers, 67
Panna cotta, honey, 163
Parfait, Greek yogurt with honey granola, 22
Pasta:
   baked with eggplant & tomatoes, 107
   baked cheese tortellini with sausage, 156
   light with lemon & garlic, 91
   salad with roasted vegetables, 123
   sardines with mushrooms & peas, 75
   zucchini with basil pesto & burrata, 118
Pide, Turkish with spiced chicken, 141
Pie, custard with figs & honey, 179
Pistachio gelato, 171
Pork tenderloin, stuffed with herbs & feta, 140

R
Ribollita soup, Tuscan with bread, 119
Rice balls, crispy with peas & herbs, 56
Rice pudding with rose petals, 175

S
Salad:
   arugula with pears & blue cheese, 115
   fennel & orange with shaved Parmesan, 98
   pasta with roasted vegetables, 123
   tuna & white bean with pepperoncini, 82
Salmon:
   grilled with Greek salad, 63
   patties with herb sauce, 74
   smoked deviled eggs, 57
Sardine toasts, smoked with orange & mint, 52
Sardines pasta with mushrooms & peas, 75
Seafood:
   paella, Spanish with shrimp & mussels, 79
   stew, rustic, 62
Shakshuka, green with spinach, 19
Sheet pan:
   garlic butter chicken & potatoes, 157
   steak gyros, 152
Shrimp in tomato & feta sauce, 70
Soup:
   artichoke with lemon & spinach, 86
   Greek lemon rice with chicken, 133
   Moroccan carrot lentil, 95
   roasted heirloom tomato gazpacho, 110
   Tuscan ribollita with bread, 119
Souvlaki, Greek chicken, 153
Spanakopita triangles, 48
Spanish omelet with potatoes, 10
Spanish seafood paella with shrimp & mussels, 79
Steak gyros, sheet pan, 152

T
Tahini sauce, green, 90
Tarts, mushroom & herbed goat cheese, 37
Toasts, smoked sardine with orange & mint, 52
Tortellini, baked cheese with sausage, 156
Tuna & white bean salad with pepperoncini, 82
Turkey meatballs in herb cream sauce, 132
Turkish dishes:
   pide with spiced chicken, 141
   scrambled eggs (Menemen), 18
Tuscan ribollita soup with bread, 119

Y
Yogurt:
   herb, 53
   herbed sauce, 32
   honey with walnuts & figs, 170
   parfait, Greek with honey granola, 22

Z
Zucchini fritters with herb yogurt, 53
Zucchini pasta with basil pesto & burrata, 118